THE ECONOMICS OF CONSTRUCTION

The Economics of Big Business

This series of books provides short, accessible introductions to the economics of major business sectors. Each book focuses on one particular global industry and examines its business model, economic strategy, the determinants of profitability as well as the unique issues facing its economic future. More general cross-sector challenges, which may be ethical, technological or environmental, as well as wider questions raised by the concentration of economic power, are also explored. The series offers rigorous presentations of the fundamental economics underpinning key industries suitable for both course use and a professional readership.

Published

The Economics of Airlines
Volodymyr Bilotkach

The Economics of Arms
Keith Hartley

The Economics of Cars
Fabio Cassia and Matteo Ferrazzi

The Economics of Construction
Stephen Gruneberg and Noble Francis

The Economics of Music
Peter Tschmuck

THE ECONOMICS OF CONSTRUCTION

STEPHEN GRUNEBERG

AND

NOBLE FRANCIS

agenda
publishing

First published in 2019 by Agenda Publishing

Agenda Publishing Limited
The Core
Bath Lane
Newcastle Helix
Newcastle upon Tyne
NE4 5TF
www.agendapub.com

ISBN 978-1-78821-014-0 (hardcover)
ISBN 978-1-78821-015-7 (paperback)

British Library Cataloguing-in-Publication Data
A catalogue record for this book is available from the British Library

Typeset by Out of House Publishing
Printed and bound in the UK by TJ International

CONTENTS

Preface   vii

1. Getting to grips with construction industry statistics:
    construction industry or construction sector?   1

2. Economic theory of markets and construction   15

3. Running a construction firm   35

4. The firm and economies of growth   61

5. Productivity and the construction market   77

6. The game of construction   95

7. The underlying causes of conflict in construction   109

8. Construction and cyclicality   119

9. Projects   145

10. The economics of construction project management   171

    Bibliography   183
    List of figures and tables   189
    Index   191

PREFACE

The construction sector shares many of its economic features with other industries but the combination of features in the construction process makes it unique. Rather than making a particular product or service for consumption, the construction sector is an enabling sector. It enables the rest of the economy to function. For example, it enables people to work in offices, make their purchases in retail outlets, travel between home and workplace by road or rail, and it provides the homes for people to bring up their families.

Construction is a highly fragmented project-based industry, with very low profit margins and a high risk of failure for the many firms operating in a very complex supply chain. In this book we try to explain how the industry functions and how the many firms throughout the supply chain collaborate on projects. We look at how construction markets operate, how firms survive in the industry, and how their business models work. We look at auctions and the tendering process and go on to discuss the construction procurement process in general, whereby construction firms are engaged by developers.

We also account for the conflicts in construction and argue that it is in the nature of the industry that disputes frequently arise in the construction process. We also discuss productivity and explain that the low productivity in construction, compared to other industries, is the price that the economy pays for a construction industry, in which business models tend to focus on the volatility of demand and managing risk at the expense of improving efficiency and productivity.

With this perspective on the construction industry, we hope that this book will enable at least some constructors to explain the reasons for the difficulties found in construction. They may then be able to give a reasonable account of their activities so that a new generation of developers and construction clients will appreciate the problems facing their contractors. Indeed, it is to be hoped that policy makers will also take note of the lessons to be found in this book when it comes to passing legislation and managing the regulation of the building process and all the firms engaged in it. This book is, therefore, written with all the key stakeholders involved in every aspect of the building and civil engineering sector in mind – from construction practitioners and policy makers to architects and site managers, from the directors of the many small- and medium-sized enterprises, often subcontractors, up to the main contractors, from the chief executives to the craft and skilled workers on site, and even to the building labourers on site, who are often the newest entrants to the industry.

Indeed, another feature of construction is that it is a labour intensive industry employing over two million people in the UK. It is a major employer of both skilled and unskilled labour and their contribution to national income is significant. There is a duty on the part of construction firms to ensure that health and safety regulations makes the construction industry improve the working conditions and treatment of its workforce. One of the distinguishing features of this book is that we include the role and contribution of the whole construction supply chain to include construction product manufacturers.

Although construction occurs in every country, the culture and practice of construction invariably has national characteristics. For example, in the UK, there is a quantity surveying profession, which generally exists in only those countries that experienced British rule at some point in their history. Even though the United States was part of the British Empire until 1783, there is no widely accepted profession as quantity surveying in the US. This book only discusses the UK construction industry although lessons can be drawn from the practice in the UK that will throw light on how the construction industries of all countries operate. The construction industry represents a microcosm of the economy and society. Its actual manifestation in the construction process varies from country to country.

While most economics text books assume that the firm is in a position to decide on the level of output in order to maximize its profits, this book highlights that this does not apply in the construction sector. In construction the level of a contractor's output is generally determined by the client or the planning constraints on site. This has implications for the relative performance of contractors, impeding their ability to obtain a similar level of profit on turnover that firms in other sectors achieve.

We have attempted to make this book more realistic than many books on the economics of the construction industry. We hope it reflects the way firms behave and gives a reasonable account for their behaviour. Misunderstanding the construction industry can lead to an undeserved criticism of the industry for its relatively low productivity compared to other sectors of the economy as well as an underestimate of the size and importance of the construction sector to the economy as a whole. In turn these misunderstandings may contribute to a poor image of the building industry and deter people from joining a vital sector of the economy, further prolonging the poor reputation of the construction industry as a consequence. We therefore seek to present construction activity, with all its shortcomings, as a necessary, vital and worthwhile economic process, essential for economic development and progress.

We begin in Chapter 1 with a survey of the data that describes the size and make up of construction in terms of the firms and specialisms within construction. This leads us on to discuss the many markets or submarkets within construction in Chapter 2. We then consider the management of firms within the industry in Chapter 3 showing how the firms have little capital compared to the value of the projects they undertake. In Chapter 4 we analyse the reasons why firms may not rest on their laurels even when they enjoy a good profitable year. To remain competitive they need to expand continually and grow. One way of achieving growth is through increasing productivity and this is discussed in Chapter 5.

We give an account of how firms navigate through the vagaries of the market place to ensure they continue to expand. One method of understanding how firms survive in the market is based on game theory and Chapter 6 provides a game theory account of the behaviour of firms. Game theory shows how firms may collaborate and also how they behave towards each other. In Chapter 7, we go on to describe the underlying causes of conflict between firms in construction (and, indeed, all sectors of the economy) to understand how divided all production processes are and yet must somehow come together for production to take place. In Chapter 8 we present an account of the irregular changes taking place in the economy, which impact on construction firms, factors that lie outside their control.

Construction is a project orientated industry with, as far as contractors are concerned, each project having a beginning, middle and end. In Chapter 9, we turn to the projects themselves and describe the nature of projects through feasibility studies, which model both the financial and non-financial costs and revenues generated by projects to assess their economic and financial viability. In Chapter 10, we conclude with a discussion of some of the approaches to managing projects adopted by the team that built the London Olympics to see what lessons might be learned from the experience gained.

While we are very grateful to Steven Gerrard at Agenda for his encouragement and support throughout the production of this book and to our families and friends for putting up with the pressures on our time in writing it, we are of course to blame for any shortcomings and errors in the book.

SG
NF

1

GETTING TO GRIPS WITH CO
INDUSTRY STATISTICS: CON!
INDUSTRY OR CONSTRUCTI(

Construction can be seen as an industry concerned with the production of the built environment. As an industry, its inputs cover a large variety of skills and materials. Its output covers many different types of products and services. As a sector of the economy, it includes the assembly of buildings and structures on site, the production of materials and building components and, indeed, the whole supply chain. This includes architects, surveyors, civil and structural engineers, plant and tool hire, construction product manufacturers and distribution. The construction sector is treated as one sector but, in fact, it covers a wide variety of work across many different areas. Construction output covers everything from the building of housing, commercial and industrial properties, education and health facilities to the building of vital infrastructure for water, energy, roads, rail, telecommunications and ports.

Whatever an individual or collection of individuals may wish or need to do in the economy or society, they will require construction to have taken place first to be able to do it. People need houses to live in, schools and universities to undertake learning, clinics and hospitals to make or keep us physically fit and comfortable, and offices to work in and shops to buy goods in. Even if we work from home and shop online then we still need the internet infrastructure to have been built. In addition, we need roads to drive on, rail infrastructure for trains to travel on, clean water for drinking and bathing, electricity and gas to power heating and lighting. As the built environment has grown over many years, the current buildings and infrastructure have developed over time, and, as a consequence, the repair, maintenance and improvement of existing buildings and infrastructure is also vital.

re the scale of investment in construction as part of the whole , the *United Kingdom National Accounts*, also known as *The Blue* (see Office for National Statistics 2017), contains a chapter entitled ross Fixed Capital Formation" (GFCF), which presents the total invested by the economy in plant and equipment and buildings and structures. This investment is essential if the country is to survive and remain competitive, in much the same way as companies need to invest in machinery in order to survive.

Fixed capital is the value of assets that usually last longer than one year and are usually used to aid production. The concept of capital formation describes the production of the means of production. The term "gross fixed capital" is used to indicate that the plant and machinery and buildings are measured at brand new values before any depreciation has been deducted.

In terms of the whole economy, investment in the built environment, which includes buildings and structures, such as infrastructure, is a vital component of the United Kingdom's fixed investment. Fixed investment is defined as long-term investment in plant and machinery, transport equipment, information technology, buildings and structures as well as major improvements to existing buildings and structures. The built environment accounts for over a half of all GFCF each year. Figure 1.1 shows that, in 2016, 52.8 per cent of all UK GFCF was in the built environment. The importance of this is that fixed investment enables increases in the productive capacity and productivity of the whole economy, by facilitating the production and movement of goods, capital, services and people.

Data covering construction

To understand a sector of the economy, you need to be able to measure it. The construction sector is certainly no exception to this. No one set of data fully explains the construction industry. However, there are three key types of official data that cover the construction sector, and each set provides a piece of the puzzle.

The first set of data is provided by the UK government's Department for Business, Energy and Industrial Strategy (BEIS) and includes all firms registered to pay value added tax (VAT), combined with an estimate of

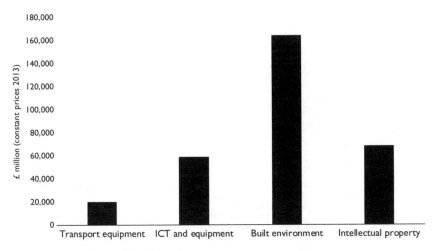

Figure 1.1 UK gross fixed capital formation (2016)
Source: ONS

very small firms that are below the VAT threshold and so do not have to pay VAT.

The benefit of this data is that it allows us to look at the basic structure of the industry. The majority of the focus tends to be on the largest firms within the construction sector. Clearly, though, the sector is dominated by small and medium-sized enterprises (SMEs), defined as firms employing fewer than 250 employees. According to the BEIS, in Figure 1.2, as much as 75 per cent of the £272 billion turnover in the construction sector in 2016 occurred within the SMEs, with 25 per cent of turnover in construction accounted for by the largest firms, which are defined as those employing 250 employees or more.

Figure 1.3 shows that the difference between large and small construction firms is even greater. Of the 2.3 million people employed in construction in 2016, 86.4 per cent were employed by SMEs, while large contractors employed only the remaining 13.6 per cent of the total construction workforce.

Furthermore, the percentage of SMEs within construction amounted to 99.9 per cent of all firms in Figure 1.4. However, a key point to note is that the largest 0.1 per cent of firms still account for 25 per cent of the total turnover of the construction industry.

The BEIS business population estimates are useful at a general level. However, they suffer from two key issues. First, the definition of construction

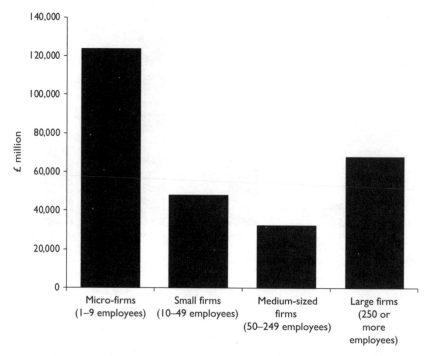

Figure 1.2 Turnover in UK construction (2016)
Source: BEIS

covers only the number of firms and employment of the contractors – those firms that operate on the construction site itself. Yet this is only one part of the whole construction supply chain, as construction is a very complex sector. Defining construction as only including contractors on site ignores the contribution of the supply chain of all the building components and materials and the design and civil and structural engineering inputs and other specialists.

Construction is a process involving architects and professionals, contractors, merchants and distributors, plant and tool hire, in addition to minerals and products manufacturers. All but the contracting element of this process is neglected in the BEIS statistics. As a result, the BEIS statistics are likely to underestimate the value of the construction sector to the UK economy.

The supply chains that supply the goods needed for on-site construction include the product manufacturers, builders' merchants and distributors, plant and tool hire. Product manufacturers produce all the materials and

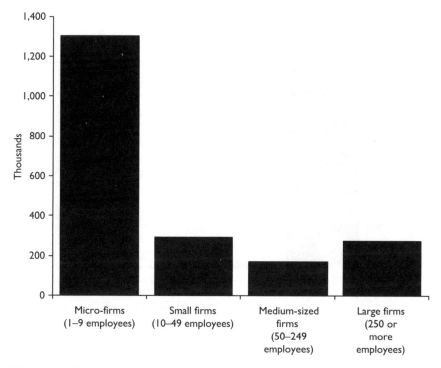

Figure 1.3 Construction employment in the UK by size of firm (2016)
Source: BEIS

products that go into the construction of a facility, and can be split into two broad categories: heavyside products and lightside products. Heavyside products include, but are not limited to, sand, bricks, concrete, asphalt, steel and glass, and tend to be used on the exterior of a building. Conversely, lightside products, which include lighting, heating and ventilation, air-conditioning and electrics, tend to be used in the interior of buildings. Builders' merchants and distributors act as wholesalers and retailers of building materials and products. Tool and plant hire firms exist to provide additional capacity for heavy machinery or tools that are needed on site to complete the project but are not currently owned by the contractor or subcontractor, which may be vital given that the bespoke nature of construction, with every end product in each project being different, means that different sets of inputs may be needed across projects. Directly owning machinery and tools for activity across all

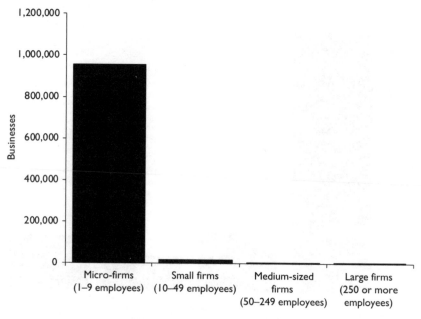

Figure 1.4 The number of firms in UK construction (2016)
Source: BEIS

areas of construction would mean considerable periods of unproductive inactivity whenever there is little work in certain sectors. It therefore makes economic sense to hire plant and machinery only when required.

In addition, even within the contracting side, there may be many layers or tiers of contractors depending upon the size of the project. For example, Figure 1.5 illustrates that, even on a small project, with only one SME contractor involved, parts of the supply chain may be hidden, including when the contractor purchases materials and products from builders' merchants and distributors and hires additional machinery and tools when needed.

However, on large projects, as in Figure 1.6, there may be more than one major contractor, operating as a joint venture, as a result of the high degree of risk and the large scale of production involved. As they are usually multi-million-pound projects, and even multi-billion-pound projects, only the largest contractors have the size to take on the risk involved. The major contractors subcontract work out to those with skills in specific areas: specialist contractors and civil engineering firms. As with machinery and tools, direct

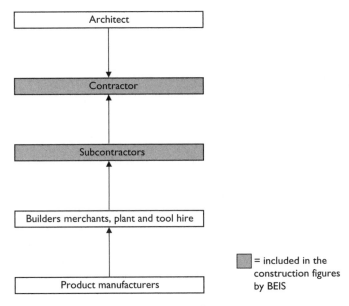

Figure 1.5 The supply chain on a small project

employment of those with specialist skills would mean significant periods of unproductive inactivity when these skills were not needed. Subcontracting out specialist skills and activities ensures that the major contractors do not suffer the burden of unproductive cost when there is a period of inactivity. At the same time, it frees up the specialist firms to find work with other main contractors, which is an efficient way of using the resources of construction firms by making it possible to have continuity of work instead of periods of idleness. Subcontracting also explains why the construction industry contains a large number of small firms, which are taken on with other subcontractors to carry out large projects. In essence, the main contractors effectively undertake the role of winning projects and managing them.

In addition, for some construction products used in large quantities, the main contractor may purchase products directly from manufacturers in order to take advantage of economies of scale or savings of size. Economies of scale exist where the purchaser can obtain a product at a lower price by purchasing large quantities because buying in bulk reduces the cost per unit.

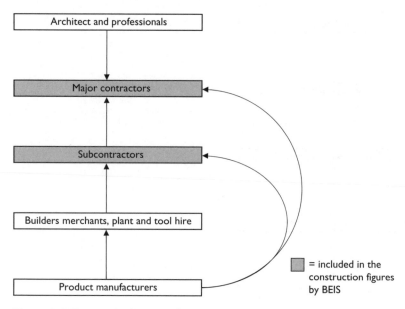

Figure 1.6 The supply chain on a large project

The Office for National Statistics (ONS) provides two other key sets of data that cover the UK construction sector. The first set of data is designed to help in calculating the total value of the output of all the industries in the economy as a whole. After steel is produced in the steel industry it is passed to the construction industry to be assembled as the steel frames of buildings. Similarly, glass is manufactured in the glass industry to become the windows as part of constructed buildings. If all the inputs to the construction industry were counted as part of the industries they come from, they would be counted twice if they were included in the value of construction output. Construction output is, therefore, only the value added to the materials and components by the contractors and subcontractors on site. Therefore, annual construction data measures only gross value added (GVA). Construction output, or construction gross value added, measures only the selling price of output minus the cost of materials, which, when taking all firms in the construction industry together, is what it provides to the UK economy after subtracting the inputs that go into construction from other industries, including designers and engineers. It is, effectively, the turnover minus the total amount spent on goods and contracted-out services. Using this method avoids double counting. Double counting would mean, for example, counting the work of subcontractors twice: once as a subcontractor, and twice when the same work was included in the value of the main contractor's sales.

Table 1.1 illustrates the GVA in UK construction during 2015, which was £119.2 billion. Sixty six per cent of this GVA was provided by building contractors, which included major contractors, specialist contractors, civil engineering contractors and the subcontractors in the construction trades. The importance of utilizing GVA rather than turnover is clear from Table 1.1, which shows that the GVA of contractors was £78.7 billion, while the total turnover or sales of contractors was £214.8 billion. Seventeen per cent of UK construction GVA is provided by manufacturers of construction products, with materials and products distribution providing 8 per cent of the GVA in the construction supply chain, while architects and professionals provide 5 per cent.

Table 1.1 The UK construction supply chain (2015)

	Gross value added £ million	Employment	Number of firms	Capital expenditure £ million	Turnover £ million
Construction products manufacturing	20,828	288,000	22,235	2,806	55,028
Building contractors	78,694	1,293,000	257,551	6,925	214,775
Materials and products distribution	9,444	194,000	10,117	1,002	43,343
Construction plant hire	3,976	43,000	3,959	1,647	5,647
Building professional services	6,222	96,000	21,187	228	8,370
Total construction	**119,164**	**1,914,000**	**315,049**	**12,608**	**327,163**

Notes: Specialized construction activities include: demolition and site preparation; electrical and plumbing installation; finishing and roofing. Building professional services includes: architects and quantity surveyors
Source: BEIS

This ONS data on construction GVA helps us to understand that what is commonly used to measure the size of the construction industry is only the contribution of contractors and subcontractors on site and not the value of the finished buildings, including the materials and all the other inputs from architects, civil and structural engineers and other construction professionals. It tells us little about the type of work undertaken in construction. Construction is therefore not really one sector but several industries, as it covers such a wide variety of work. However, the second type of data available from the ONS covering the construction sector can give us an insight into the different areas of activity within the construction sector and how it varies over time.

This information comes from the "Monthly Business Survey (for Construction and Allied Trades)", which measures construction output from the industry in the UK. The survey samples 8,000 businesses, which include all businesses either employing over 100 people or with an annual turnover of more than £60 million. Construction output is defined as the amount chargeable to customers for building and civil engineering work done in the period, excluding taxes. However, once again, businesses are asked to exclude any subcontracted work, to avoid counting the work of subcontractors twice: once when the subcontractors record the value of their work in their statistics, but not when it might otherwise be included by the main contractors as part of the value of their output. Construction output also does not include payments made to architects or professionals from other firms. However, it would include them if they were directly employed by a contracting business registered in construction.

The ONS construction output data allows us to look at the value of construction output at current prices, which includes inflation. Current prices are the prices charged by contractors, and, over time, these prices increase because of inflation. Inflation is the steady loss in the value of money because of firms raising their prices, as the same quantity of output is sold for a higher price. If inflation is removed from the data, construction output can be measured in constant prices, showing the actual change in the quantity of construction activity.

Figure 1.7 illustrates the time series of construction output at both current and constant prices. The value of construction at constant prices helps us to assess the real change in output. The value data shows that the total value may have increased over time but it does not inform us whether the

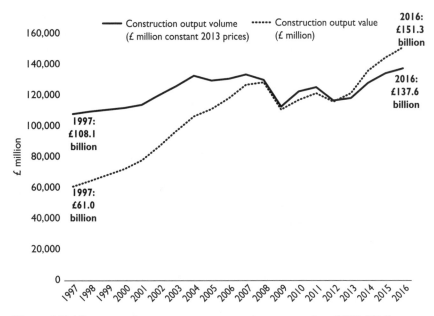

Figure 1.7 UK construction output at current and constant prices (1997–2016)
Source: ONS

change is attributable to price increases or to increases in the real volume of construction. In Figure 1.7, between 1997 and 2007 the value of construction output more than doubled, an increase of 108 per cent. However, the volume of construction output rose by only 24 per cent. Consequently, the majority of the growth in construction value over the 1997–2007 period was attributable to increases in price. Over the same period UK economic activity grew by 34 per cent, so UK construction did not increase as quickly as the rest of the country's economy.

One reason the construction industry did not grow when the rest of the economy expanded may have been because, every year during this period, the construction industry produced sufficient output not only to replace the existing stock of buildings and infrastructure but also to add to the building stock needed to accommodate expansion in the economy, and the increase in stock was achieved without increasing construction output by as large a percentage increase as the rest of the economy. One reason for this possibility is that buildings and infrastructure are durable. Once built they may last many decades, and annual construction output can easily exceed the amount of building work needed to maintain the current stock, a proportion of which constantly needs demolition and replacing.

During the financial crisis the value of construction output at current prices fell by 6.5 per cent between 2008 and 2009. However, after inflation has been removed from the figures, the volume of construction activity fell by 17.8 per cent between 2007 and 2009. This contrasts sharply with a 5.1 per cent fall in UK national income over the same period, evidence that the UK construction industry was three times more volatile than the UK economy overall. The volatility of construction activity is a subject we return to in a later chapter, as it greatly influences the need to cope with sharply fluctuating demand and uncertainty in the construction industry.

The second reason that this ONS data is useful is that it allows us to look at the structure of the construction sector by activity, breaking down total construction output into its components such as housing, infrastructure and commercial buildings or into new build and repair and maintenance. The ONS data is broken down by different construction sectors, illustrated by the value of output in 2016 (Figure 1.8). The largest sectors of activity in construction

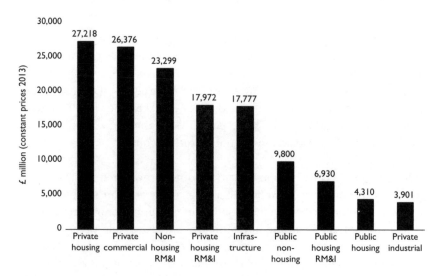

Figure 1.8 UK construction output by sector (2016)
Source: ONS

are the £27.2 billion private housing sector and the £26.4 billion commercial sector, which includes offices, retail, hotels and privately financed education and health, all of which the ONS also provides data for. The third largest construction sector is the £18 billion private housing repair, maintenance and improvement (RM&I) sector, which is – surprisingly – larger than the £17.8 billion infrastructure sector. The private housing RM&I sector covers a broad range of work on existing private residences and includes everything from repairing a boiler or electrical wiring to adding an extension or building a conservatory. Each individual project in private housing RM&I is relatively small but, given that there were 28.5 million homes in the UK during 2016 and 37 per cent of the existing homes were built before the Second World War, the aggregation of all these small projects is substantial. The ONS splits the infrastructure sector into subsectors covering water and sewerage, roads, rail, energy, gas, air and communications, in addition to harbours and waterways. The public non-housing sector was worth £6.9 billion in 2016 and includes publicly funded education, health, prisons and defence-related construction. Industrial construction covers the building of new factories and warehouses. Overall, repair and maintenance of both housing and other buildings and structures accounted for over one-third (35 per cent) of total construction in 2016 and is larger than any of the individual sectors covering the construction of new facilities. This reflects the fact that the economic and social value of existing buildings and structures is relatively high, but the cost of demolishing them and rebuilding new is also high. As a consequence, it is worthwhile for the owners of the buildings and structures to invest in repairing, maintaining and improving existing facilities to offset the depreciation in their value.

Within these sectors, there are two different types of construction: build to order and speculative build. The majority of construction activity is funded directly by a client ordering a building or structure that meets their specifications. This may be publicly funded or privately funded. Speculative building cannot be certain of a profit from the sale of the building as no price has been agreed in advance. The key difference between building to order and speculative building is that building to order implies an agreement to build and be paid for a project in return for a known sum of money. Speculative building involves taking on the considerable risks associated with finding a demand to meet the supplied building or structure, which in general means selling the building or structure to a customer or finding a customer to utilize the building or structure that the speculator owns. As a result, these speculators are developers. Although speculative building is not the majority of construction, it is prevalent in the two largest construction sectors: private housing and private commercial.

Concluding remarks

The construction industry covers the activity of building across many different sectors to ensure that the facilities exist to provide the basis for everything that an economy needs: housing, schools and hospitals, offices and factories, roads, railways, airports and utilities such as water, energy and telecommunications. The construction of all these facilities requires many different firms to ensure that the vast array of skills and products are available. However, the high risk involved in major projects also means that the industry is highly fragmented, with large firms spreading risk by subcontracting out activity to many subcontractors on each project. Measuring all these activities is very complex, and it requires the use of a variety of data sources to understand the structure of the industry.

2

ECONOMIC THEORY OF MARKETS AND CONSTRUCTION

The basic underpinnings of economic theory are essential to understand how the construction sector works. However, although concepts such as demand and supply, which are a key part of standard economic theory, are necessary in order to view the construction sector, they are not sufficient on their own given the complexity of the industry.

An introduction to supply and demand and market competition helps to highlight the differences between construction and other sectors of the economy. A description of how markets actually operate in construction demonstrates a more realistic account of what can be observed in the building industry compared to a simple theoretical repetition of supply and demand, which nevertheless still contributes to an understanding of construction and property markets.

The laws of demand and supply can be used to illustrate how a market for any product operates. In this simplification or model of the world, there are only two groups of people: those on the supply side and those on the demand side. The first group are those willing and able to produce and sell a product or service. They organize production and sell the finished output. Organizing the production process means bringing together or combining the various elements that need to be used in the production process. This means bringing the factors of production or different types of resources together to manufacture or construct a building or structure. The factors of production consist of four categories. They are land, labour, capital and enterprise, although many people have argued that there are only three factors of production, namely land, capital and labour, and some have even argued that there are only two factors of production, land and capital. Land, as a factor of production, includes the location where production takes place and the mineral resources under the surface. The construction industry is unusual when compared with most industries in that contractors do not usually own or rent the location of the site where their work takes place, except for their head offices. It is the developer who purchases the site and hires the contractor to build for them. The return to land as a factor of production is rent.

Economic rent is defined as the payment for a factor of production over and above what that factor could earn in an alternative use. As the use of land cannot easily be switched between different uses, there is no ready alternative and, therefore, all the income the owner of land receives is economic rent. This idea of economic rent extends to the other factors of production and stems from the fact that the price of a factor of production is derived from the competition between employers to take on workers. If a worker could earn £500 per week in alternative employment but was earning £700 per week in their current job, then their income included an economic rent of £200. If they had only received £500 per week they would not have charged their employer an economic rent.

Labour is the human factor of production that ensures that goods and services are transformed from raw materials to finished goods and services. One feature of labour as a factor of production is that it involves spending time in the production process.

Capital is a factor of production as it is used to purchase materials, labour, plant and other resources prior to the receipt of revenues from the sale of the finished article or service. It can take the form of financial assets but also includes real estate, stocks of materials and finished produce or products.

Enterprise is often seen as a factor of production in some economics textbooks because there is a need to have a catalyst to enable production. The motive of the entrepreneur is assumed to be profit, the reward for taking the risk of setting up the enterprise or project. The return to enterprise as a factor of production is therefore profit.

The second group of people are those on the demand side. They are willing and able to purchase the product or service. Demand is the quantity that people are willing and able to buy. The quantity demanded depends on a number of factors, including the price of the product, the income of individuals or the budgets of firms, the taste of buyers, the price of alternatives and other goods and services.

The first law of demand states that the higher the price of a product, the less will be demanded. This intuitively makes sense, assuming that nothing else changes – or, as economists put it, *ceteris paribus*, which, literally translated from Latin, means "other things being equal". The lower the price of a product, the more people can afford it and therefore want to purchase it.

Similarly, the law of supply states that the higher the price of a product, the more people will be willing to make and sell it, *ceteris paribus*. The lower the price, fewer people will be willing and able to take on the task of making and supplying the product. In the homes example, if homes were to cost £10 million each, then more people would be happy to build and sell them, *ceteris paribus*. Given the same costs and other economic conditions, these groups would be making more profit from the high price. However, if homes were only £100,000 each, fewer people would be willing to build and supply them, *ceteris paribus*, assuming that costs and other factors in the economy were to remain the same. Furthermore, using the example of bricks, a higher price of bricks would mean that, *ceteris paribus*, there would be more people willing to make and supply bricks, as they would be able to increase their revenue.

Figure 2.1 shows the interaction of the two groups in the market, those wishing to sell and those wishing to purchase. Price is measured on the vertical axis and quantity on the horizontal axis. As the price increases, so does the quantity supplied, as shown by line S, while the quantity demanded declines, as shown by line D, assuming everything else remains the same. This reflects the argument that the lower the price of the product, the greater the quantity demanded. Meanwhile, line S illustrates how supply changes when prices change: the higher the price of the product, the higher the supply. As a result, the supply line is upward-sloping.

The point at which these two lines intersect is what economists call equilibrium, where the forces of supply and demand are in balance. At the equilibrium price there is no shortage or surplus and, in theory, there is no reason for price to change. At this price the demand for the product matches the supply. At price P_e, suppliers are willing to make and supply quantity Q_e of the product. At the same time, those who can and wish to purchase the product are willing to pay P_e for the quantity Q_e on offer. As a consequence, there is no need for suppliers to make and sell any more or fewer. In addition, there is no need for those who wish to purchase to go without the product.

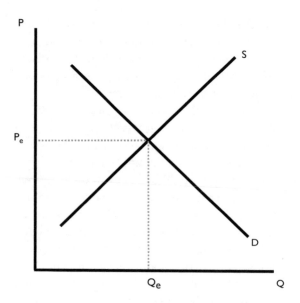

Figure 2.1 Simple supply and demand showing price equilibrium

At prices above the equilibrium, more would be offered for sale than consumers wished to buy, and a surplus would arise. The existence of a surplus places a downward pressure on prices, to rid the market of the excess. At prices below the equilibrium there would be shortages, and prices would rise as consumers competed to purchase whatever was available on the market.

Of course, only those with sufficient money or a high enough income would be able to participate in the market. Those without the ability to pay do not participate in the market. This is important to bear in mind, as many people cannot afford to buy food and instead are reliant on charity or food banks in order to survive. This is an example of market failure. In a similar manner, within the housing market, many people may not be able to buy or rent a house as the prices are too great for them to make a realistic offer. Otherwise, such people are excluded from the market and cannot participate except through family or government intervention on their behalf.

Surpluses and shortages are shown in Figure 2.2. If suppliers tried to charge P_2, which is above the equilibrium price, the quantity on offer would be greater than the quantity buyers were willing or able to purchase. Supply

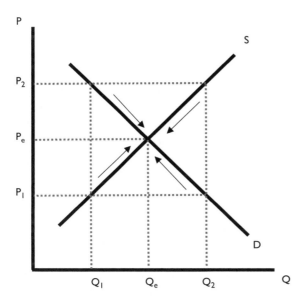

Figure 2.2 The market mechanism

would increase to Q_2, but buyers would wish to purchase only Q_1, which would lead to an excess supply or a surplus of unsold output equivalent to Q_2–Q_1. As a result, firms would reduce their prices to attract more buyers and sell enough to remove the surplus by reducing the price. This is the case at any point above price P_e.

Similarly, if the market price of a product is below the equilibrium, at, say, P_1, then fewer firms would wish to supply the product. This situation arises because firms are in competition with each other. They do not necessarily know what their competitors are producing and, taken together, they may all make similar decisions to produce at the same time, creating a surplus in the process.

For example, in the London commercial property market, when the return on investment in offices is low, it follows that property prices are high and the returns reflect the low risk of property investment. In such a market developers may see an opportunity to develop a site and sell into the high-price office market at what appears to be an attractive profit. The same market signals appeal to several developers at the same time, and their reaction to the market leads them to invest in property developments simultaneously. Their responses combine to form a wave of development that then comes onto the market in the space of a few months, after a time lag caused by the time it takes to build the offices.

The resulting surplus of offices causes long periods of time when office buildings remain empty on completion. This surplus of empty offices can cause office rents to decline, although often this takes the form of attractive deals for any firms willing to occupy an office block, for example, with rent-free periods. As the capital value of a built asset depends on its rent, developers and banks are reluctant to reduce the nominal rent charged, which, therefore, makes it difficult to recognize that rents have fallen as a consequence of excess supply. Prices will drop only as a last resort. Nevertheless, the basic economic theory reveals what is actually taking place in the market over time.

Given a price of P_1 (in Figure 2.2), firms would wish to make and supply only Q_1 units of the product. At such a low price, the demand would rise to Q_2. However, this quantity does not exist, and there is now a shortage. Firms can use the shortage to charge higher and higher prices. These higher prices lead to a fall in people being able to purchase at any price below P_e, and as they drop out of the market the shortage in the market disappears. When the price is below the equilibrium, suppliers will continue to raise prices, and buyers will continue to outbid other buyers until the price reaches P_e, where there is no shortage or surplus.

In a food market, for example, if food prices rise to the equilibrium it does not mean that those people who could not afford food before the price rise can now be fed. It simply means that the quantity of food available for sale is equivalent to the quantity of food those who can afford it are willing to buy. Although the shortage in the market may have disappeared, the higher prices do not mean that those who cannot afford to buy can now feed their families. It means simply that the quantity people are willing and able to buy is the same as the quantity firms are willing and able to sell. Similarly, a rise in house prices does not solve the problem of homelessness, unless government intervention builds more houses in the public sector or adopts policies that encourage private developers to build.

This general description of how markets operate illustrates the market over-all. However, to gain an insight into how firms operate within markets we turn to a theoretical firm in a perfectly competitive market. Once it is understood, the simplifying assumptions can be relaxed. This is not an attempt to describe the real world; it is an attempt to understand how firms behave.

The simplest type of market is called the perfectly competitive market. A perfectly competitive market depends on four conditions. First, all products or services on sale must be identical. If the product or service is not identical, then the buyer may have preferences, with the result that firms are not in competition.

Second, there must be many buyers and sellers. Each firm is therefore only a minor part of the market, and its small percentage of sales in the market implies that it has no influence over price. As a result, every firm in perfect competition is a price taker, not a price maker.

Third, there has to be freedom to enter or leave the market. There are no barriers to entry or exit. In a perfectly competitive market, new competitors are free to offer their product or service without hindrance of any sort. This means that, when a market becomes profitable for any reason, new firms will be able to enter and increase the quantity that firms are willing and able to supply.

Finally, the fourth condition of perfect competition is perfect knowledge. This includes all competitors having full knowledge of the technologies involved, the sourcing of materials and even the list of potential customers. There can be no trade secrets in perfect competition. Otherwise, it would be possible to fool the buyers. In any case, all buyers in a perfectly competitive market would also share full knowledge of the product or service, so that it would not be possible to overcharge a customer.

All four conditions are needed, otherwise the market is not perfectly competitive. The term "perfect" means "absolute". It is not a value judgement indicating approval. The reason for setting out the conditions of perfect competition is that only when all the conditions have been met are the profits of firms reduced to the minimum necessary to make production worthwhile but without making above-normal profits. Normal profits are set at a level just high enough not to attract more competitors and not so low that firms decide to leave the market. At this level of profit the market is stable in terms of the number of suppliers and buyers and the quantities bought and sold.

Taken together with the equilibrium price, the conditions of perfect competition ensure that firms produce at their most efficient level of output and the market remains stable. Unfortunately, perfect competition is an impossible state of affairs, if only because perfect knowledge is impossible to achieve in any market. Moreover, there are always changes taking place, giving rise to opportunities for firms to take advantage of the circumstances at the expense of their competitors. Finally, because firms in perfect competition do not all face the same costs, some will be more profitable than others; for example, those closer to the market have lower transport costs than those in the best position. As a result of these different costs, the most efficient firms will generate higher profits than others, and as a result will be in a position to take over smaller, less efficient competitors. This ultimately leads to markets being dominated by the most successful firms, which eventually dominate the market, and the market can no longer be said to be perfectly competitive.

Returning to the economic theory of the firm in perfect competition, it can be argued that, although the demand curve for the market as a whole is downward-sloping, for any particular firm in perfect competition it is horizontal. This is because, if any one firm, *ceteris paribus*, tries to raise its prices, those who wish to purchase the product will simply go to the other firms, where the price is now somewhat lower. The customers can do this because they have perfect knowledge. It is unlikely that a firm in a perfectly competitive market would want to reduce its price, as it can already sell all its output at the going rate. As a consequence, any individual firm takes its price from the general market. It is a price taker.

At this point, a digression is necessary to discuss the costs and revenues of firms. Accountants and economists look at costs and revenues but ask different questions. Accountants want to know what the tax liabilities of a firm are, what the profits had been for the benefit of shareholders and how a firm's performance might compare to its competitors. Economists ask different questions, such as: how do firms maximize profits? What level of output produces the greatest profit? Is the firm efficient? In truth, the answers to these questions are also of interest to accountants. The point is that, whereas accountants traditionally consider the accounts of firms after the trading period has ended, economists have tended to focus on questions concerned with management issues and the decision-making processes of running a firm, and hence they tend to look at questions with a view to the future development of the firm.

To assist in decision-making, economists consider costs and revenues using the following method. All costs either vary as output expands or remain the same. A cost that changes with output is a variable cost (VC), and includes materials and labour. A cost that remains the same when output changes is called a fixed cost (FC), and includes rent, interest on past borrowing and head office costs when staff are paid the same rate regardless of the quantity produced. Some labour is therefore an FC while the pay of other workers is a VC. Adding fixed costs to variable costs gives total cost (TC). Dividing total cost by output gives total cost per unit, or unit cost or average cost (AC). For example, if the total cost of building ten houses is £10 million, then the AC is £1 million.

The final cost to be considered is the marginal cost (MC). The concept of MC is extremely important, as it defines how firms generate profits. MC is the additional cost of one additional product. For example, if the total cost of ten houses is £10 million and the total cost of 11 houses is £10.5 million, then the MC of the 11th house is £500,000. It is quite likely that materials and labour are available to use as a result of having spare materials and capacity from the first ten houses. In this case, there may well be some available for the 11th house, which reduces the MC of the 11th house.

Turning to the revenue side, the horizontal demand line in Figure 2.3 shows that those wishing to purchase are willing to pay only the going rate, not a penny more, and the firms in perfect competition can sell all the produce at the going rate and do not need to reduce their price in order to sell their total output. Only at the going rate (P_e) are buyers and sellers willing to agree the price. The average revenue (AR) is the total revenue divided by the total number sold. The marginal revenue (MR) is the change in total revenue that the firm gains from producing and selling one more unit. The total revenue (TR) is the number of houses multiplied by their price, assuming that all are sold at the same price. If everything is sold at the same price, the AR is TR divided by the number of units sold. Finally, MR is the change in TR as a result of selling one more unit.

The relationship between AR and MR is important, because it demonstrates the difference that changing output by even one unit can make to profits. The relationship between AR and MR is the same as the relationship between the water in a bath and the water coming out of the hot water tap. If left for long enough, the temperature of the bath water cools. If the temperature in the pipes has cooled down, turning on the hot tap does not instantly flow with hot water, but soon the water in the tap begins to heat up and flow warmer than the water in the bath, and therefore the tap water soon raises

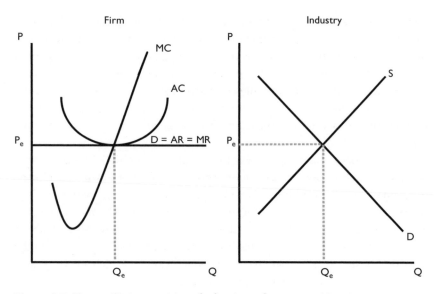

Figure 2.3 The equilibrium position of a firm in perfect competition

the temperature of the water in the bath. Similarly, if the MC is lower than the AC the MC pulls the AC down, and when the MC is above the AC it pulls the AC up. If we apply these definitions of costs and revenues to the management of a firm, such as a house builder, then the marginal revenue is the change in total revenue when one more house is built and sold. If the total revenue from the sale of ten houses is £12 million and the total revenue from the sale of 11 houses is £12,700,000, an increase of £700,000, then the MR of the 11th house is £700,000. In this case, by building the 11th house, the house builder has made an additional contribution to the firm of £200,000, namely the MR of £700,000 less the MC of £500,000, adding to the profits of the firm. The contribution to the firm's profits is found by subtracting the MC of the 11th house from the MR of the 11th house. As long as the firm is making additional contributions by building additional housing units, it is adding to the profits of the firm each time it adds additional units of production; it adds to the profits up to a certain point, beyond which the return on each additional house sale eventually begin to decline. This is because the marginal cost increases and approaches the value of the marginal revenue, squeezing the excess from each sale. This is known as the law of diminishing returns. When the additional cost of the last sale is equal to the additional revenue the firm will have maximized the profits it can make. It has found its profit-maximizing level of output. Further sales would mean that the additional costs would be greater than the additional revenues. Profit-maximizing firms will attempt to produce when the MR of the last unit sold is equal to the MC of the last unit built – at Q_e in Figure 2.3.

The end result is a stable equilibrium, any deviation from which soon leads to a return to equilibrium, as it is not in the interest of the firms to produce more or less. This gives a basic framework that helps in understanding how markets operate. However, perfect competition is a simplification and requires some large assumptions about the market, many of which are unrealistic for a sector as complex as construction in the real world.

Within construction, the product is rarely generic. Almost all buildings and structures in construction are completely bespoke, whether it be a house, refurbishment project, school, hospital, office, shop, factory, warehouse, road, rail track or power station. Within a single block of apartments, flats may be very similar, but different blocks of apartments will be bespoke.

Although housing and commercial offices are speculative developments with many possible customers, the majority of construction remains client-driven. Often there is only one buyer, with the client/developer determining the contract to build to a specific design. Conversely, on the producer side of the equation, for many specific types of construction, such as infrastructure, there are very few large contractor firms with the skills to compete for and win the contract for and build the structure. Within product manufacturing, the high total costs of production due to the use of capital machinery and technology mean that, to ensure the average costs of production are low, there are likely to be only a few large firms producing high volumes.

Aspects of perfect competition exist in construction. For example, the free entry and exit of firms may apply to certain kinds of construction work. Small contractors working on small repair, maintenance and improvement construction projects have low costs of entry into the industry. In the UK, many small contractors do not have to be professionally qualified and registered. However, the majority of projects in construction involve considerable amounts of inputs such as labour, capital machinery, funding and the experience to win the contract, and these all form barriers to entry for small firms.

The high degree of uncertainty in construction, because each project is unique, means that there is also a high degree of risk involved for the producer in terms of both building and selling, especially given the large extent of subcontracting. There is also a high degree of risk involved for the client. One possible method of reducing this risk is to ensure long-term relationships when possible. Working with the same set of subcontractors allows for improvements in productivity over time as groups of specialist firms and workers begin to understand each other better. When clients of the industry engage with the construction process and the consortium of firms in the construction supply chain, there is an increased probability of projects meeting the specification and the original intention of the client. However, main contractors and clients tend to rely on market testing to ensure they obtain specialist skills at the best possible price, sometimes at the expense of disrupting the construction team. Market testing is the practice of asking a small number of firms to tender for a work package. Projects are broken down into work packages that specify the work to be carried out. A work package is therefore a defined amount of work.

At the other end of the market spectrum from perfect competition is monopoly. In a monopoly market there is only one producer in a market for a specific product or specialist skill. As there is only one firm selling, the firm and the industry are one and the same thing. At the same time, there are significant barriers to entry, which may be a result of high costs, limited inputs, technical specifications or quality issues. In this case, rather than being a price taker, the monopolist is a price maker. Without competition, the monopolist firm is in a position to determine its own price to its customers, ensuring that it makes profits at their expense. Unlike perfect competition, it faces a downward-sloping demand curve, and the marginal revenue is not equal to the average revenue. This is because, if the firm wants to sell more, then it can but it must reduce the price of all output, reducing the average revenue per unit. However, like a firm in perfect competition, in theoretical terms the monopolist still chooses to produce the output level where MC is the same as MR. This is highlighted in Figure 2.4. But at this level of output the price the firm receives for each unit, P_e, is higher than the price under perfect competition and the average cost. This difference is the profit that a monopolist earns, which is far greater than it would make if it faced real competition. In the absence of competition, monopolies are left to

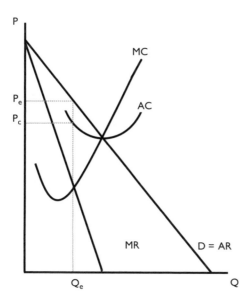

Figure 2.4 A monopoly

charge what they wish. They tend to restrict output and raise price. For this reason, monopolistic profits are seen as not being in the public interest, and the Monopolies and Mergers Commission was set up in the UK in 1949 to deal with the issues of protecting the public interest in respect to monopoly markets. The Monopolies Commission was replaced by the Competition Commission in 1998, which was itself renamed the Competition and Markets Authority (CMA) in 2014.

A third market type is oligopoly, in which only a few firms compete with each other to supply their goods and services. This is the most common type of market of all, as most markets are dominated by a few large firms, even when there are many small firms in the market too. For example, although there are many shops selling groceries, the market is dominated by a few well-known large supermarkets. In construction, the industry is highly fragmented by trade and region. The result is that in any one regional market there are only a few large firms, such as electrical engineers or plumbing firms, with many small firms. The largest firms undertake the largest projects in their area while the smaller firms compete for the numerous smaller jobs that become available. Often the smallest firms are employed by the larger firms, when needed on particular projects, when the smallest firms are called sub-subcontractors.

In oligopolistic markets the firms compete with each other, but not on price. The reason is that, if a firm chooses to cut its prices, the other firms will follow suit and cut their prices too. This destroys the advantage the first mover was hoping for, namely to charge less than the competitors and gain some of their market share. On the other hand, if the firm raises its price, the other firms will hold their prices steady in the hope that customers of the first firm move to those firms that have held their prices steady. The reactions of the other firms in oligopolistic competition are designed to gain market share at the expense of the first mover, and this expected behaviour acts as a deterrent to making price changes. This is not to say that there is little competition in oligopoly, but it is not price competition. Non-price competition can be based on quality, service and public image or a combination of all three. For this reason oligopolistic firms often have large advertising budgets and sponsor sporting and other cultural events. More recently larger firms have invested in corporate social responsibility, to show they have concerns, for example, about the environment, sustainability and public welfare, in order to raise their public profile and image even in the construction sector.

For smaller construction projects, such as repair, maintenance or refurbishment projects, there are still many firms in the market, including architecture practices and smaller contractors. However, on larger-scale projects, the large requirements for labour, capital machinery and up-front finance mean that there are considerably fewer architectural and contractor firms available for and capable of taking on the risks and management involved. The size distribution of firms in construction mirrors the size distribution of building projects. The vast majority of building projects and work packages in construction are relatively small. Even the largest of projects are split up into smaller work packages or parts of a building project, in order to enable smaller firms to take on the work and the risks involved, even when a major contractor has committed to taking on a very large project.

This approach to undertaking large projects contrasts with the production of construction products, which require high up-front capital investment in large manufacturing facilities, machinery and technology to make products efficiently and take advantage of economies of scale, mentioned in Chapter 1. In construction product manufacturing, the largest firms are able to invest in, and make full use of, machinery and technology, effective management, savings through purchasing in bulk and greater sales through marketing and public relations, as well as having greater availability through mass production and cheaper finance through borrowing large sums from financial institutions or listing on stock markets.

However, this does not take into account the inflexibility of plant and machinery and its limited capacity, without significant investment, available to manufacturers. Altering the size of the production line takes time in order to increase the capacity of firms to increase production. There is a delay, for example, before brick producers can respond to changing market conditions to manufacture the additional bricks, which may involve taking plant out of resting. Of course, manufacturers may hold stocks of bricks in reserve to deal with fluctuations in demand. These stocks are referred to in economics as inventories. Firms use inventories to smooth production over time. When stocks are insufficient to meet demand, firms may also decide to import bricks to deal with fluctuations in demand at home. This can be seen in Figure 2.5, which shows the relationship between all construction materials imports and construction

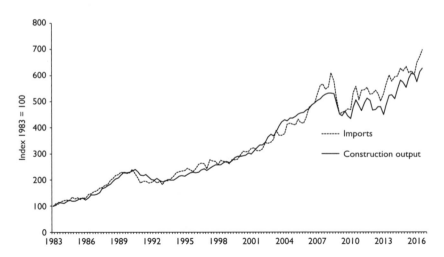

Figure 2.5 Index of UK imports and construction output (1983–2016)
Source: ONS

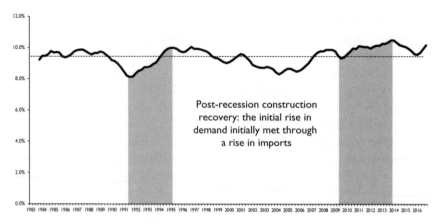

Figure 2.6 UK imports of construction materials as a proportion of construction output (1983–2016)
Source: ONS, BEIS

output. Both series are indexed to 100 in 1983 Q1 for comparison purposes, and the chart illustrates the change in both imports and construction output over time. Figure 2.5 shows the constant dependence on imports of construction materials to meet construction output demand over the long term.

The size of the construction industry is much greater than the value of imported materials but the figure compares how these two very different variables change in line with each other. In Figure 2.6, imports of construction products as a proportion of total construction output are illustrated over the same time period, showing that the ratio has been relatively stable in the long term, again illustrating the close relationship between construction materials imports and construction output. Imports have accounted for 9.4 per cent of construction output on average, varying only between 8 and 11 per cent since 1983. However, a further key point is that Figure 2.6 also illustrates the extent to which the UK has been dependent on imports of materials to make up for a shortfall in domestic capacity. This has tended to occur in years in which imports have expanded more than construction output. In effect, the times when imports as a proportion of construction output have risen the most were in the post-recessionary periods, showing how imports are able to respond to increases in demand more rapidly than domestic production.

Technology

This chapter has focused on traditional economic theory and standard business models in construction based around making and selling a product or building. However, a key significant structural change in the global economy over the last 30 years has been the use of technology and the internet, not merely to improve productivity and automate standard jobs but to enable new business models. These new business models do not involve making a product or providing a direct service. Instead, they enable the sharing of underutilized existing resources and the utilization of technology to connect people – and their existing resources that are not being used – with people who wish to use those resources but find that it is not cost-effective to purchase and own the resources.

Other parts of the economy have already seen these business models develop. The most high-profile examples of this are in the people transportation industry, with Uber taking the lead, and in the accommodation sector, where Airbnb is the most high-profile example. Uber, Airbnb and other similar firms then connect the two actors, the provider and the purchaser, allocating the resources in an efficient manner. Uber does not own any taxis and Airbnb does not own any accommodation, so their costs are low compared with existing taxi and accommodation providers. Uber merely allows people to utilize their cars when they may have previously been unused and Airbnb allows people to rent out their unused rooms, flats or houses on a short-term basis, both providing a rate of return that would not have been possible otherwise. Uber and Airbnb then take a small proportion of the return. The incentive in this tech business model is to have as many transactions as possible and, as a consequence, as many people supplying taxi services or accommodation for Uber and Airbnb, respectively, in addition to having as many people as possible registered with them who would be interested in using taxis or accommodation.

Although the actors involved in taxi rides, on both the demand and supply sides, have always existed, the internet and technology have reduced the cost and greatly increased the ease with which these two actors can connect. The apps are available on smartphones, which the majority of people now have. They are also free and easy to use, with maps to locate those closest, cheapest and/or quickest, all to incentivize more people to use them. Online rating systems and social networks increase the access to information on the trust-worthiness of both those supplying the services and those demanding the services. Internet payment systems also make it easier to pay for such services.

The key question is: what is the impact of such business models on firms that operate using traditional business models but supplying a similar good or service? Zervas, Proserpio and Byers (2017) analysed the impact of Airbnb on the hotel sector in the state of Texas. The results of their analysis indicate that the impact of Airbnb on revenue in the hotel sector varies by geographic area and by type of hotel. On average, in Austin, the capital, where the supply of rooms through Airbnb supply is highest, the overall impact has been a decrease in hotel revenue of up to 10 per cent. In addition, the impact has been greatest in periods of peak demand, such as during conferences and festivals, when Airbnb's supply can instantaneously increase in response to a substantial change in demand. Moreover, the impact on traditional hotel revenue is greatest for low-price budget hotels. Conversely, there was a significantly lower impact on hotels that are aiming at business travellers for whom the focus is not purely on cost but also on additional facilities that hotels may provide.

Wallsten (2015) explored the competitive effects of Uber on the taxi industry, and, controlling for underlying trends, finds that the introduction of Uber into the transportation market led to a significant decline in trips taken using traditional taxis. In addition, the research also finds that the introduction, and increasing use, of Uber has led to a reduction in the number of complaints in connection with traditional taxi trips, as people choose to switch from traditional taxis to Uber in response to poor service. Prior to Uber there were no other competitive options.

What it is difficult to predict at this stage is how these new business models will infiltrate the construction industry. Twenty years ago it would have been difficult to predict the rise of Uber and Airbnb and the extent to which they have disrupted existing business models. Uber was started in August 2008 and Airbnb was started in March 2009, yet by 2017 Uber had a revenue of $7.5 billion and Airbnb's revenue was $2.6 billion. What is clear is that the business models are new, enabled by easy-to-use technology and focusing on the utilization of existing assets. As a consequence, in the building industry the key areas that have potential to lend themselves to the disruptive use of technology are construction plant hire and tool hire and online purchasing and auctions. Currently subcontractors find that plant and many tools are too expensive to purchase outright, especially when they will be used only sporadically. As a result, the majority of firms hire plant and tools for specific projects from firms whose sole purpose is to hold and rent out plant and tools. Yet, if subcontractors were able to – in an easy manner in which they can have trust – hire plant and tools from other firms that do own such plant or tools but may not be using them on their current project, then they would be able to do so at a considerably lower rate than from a dedicated plant or tool hire firm. If new-tech business models are successful in construction, then examples from other sectors such as Uber and Airbnb suggest that traditional players in the plant and tool hire parts of the construction supply chain could suffer from a significant loss in revenue and employment in the medium term.

At this stage it is far from certain that these tech disruptor business models will have a great impact on the construction industry. The focus of such business models has been on successes such as Uber and Airbnb. However, these business models have been extended to rental schemes for sectors as varied as bicycles, dog kennel services, boat rentals, photographic equipment, musical instruments and garden equipment, with varied levels of success and many failures. The most successful rent-sharing business models have tended to begin with a relatively small area, a city or region, which is then expanded to cover multiple cities and countries. In 2017 Uber covered 663 cities world-wide while Airbnb covered 65,000 cities in 192 countries. The business models have also tended to be focused on enabling new businesses and their interactions with consumers who are focused on cost, location and flexibility rather than other businesses. Within construction, if the key impact is likely to be on the more efficient utilization of plant or tool hire, then this implies it will be focused on business-to-business interactions, which constitute an area in which the tech business models have so far been less successful. However, given that 86 per cent of employment in construction is within small and medium-sized enterprises, their focus may primarily be on cost, location and flexibility rather than other features that larger firms may be interested in.

So far these business models have benefited from a lack of regulation and a legal framework, which have developed to deal with previous business models based around providing a direct product or service, such as taxi firms and hotels. As we are currently in the process of developing these new models, it may be that the regulatory and legal frameworks will adjust, in time, and provide these new business models with regulation that makes them come in line with traditional business models. If this is the case, it is likely to provide the tech business models with less of a return, and, as a result, it may mean that there is less investment in such business models.

Concluding remarks

The key economic concepts of supply and demand give us a clear insight into how markets operate and the motivations for firms within an industry sector. Economic analysis of how markets operate shows how buyers compete with each other to bid up prices when there is not enough to satisfy the requirements, demonstrating how competition between firms reduces prices when firms undercut the prices offered by their competitors in order to win orders and sales. However, the assumptions in economic models are often highly constraining, and there are often external factors that can affect the workings of these models. These constraints, in addition to economies of scale, go a long way to explaining why many parts of the construction supply chain lend themselves to having just a few large firms.

3

RUNNING A CONSTRUCTION FIRM

In this chapter, costs and revenues and basic accounts are used to show how firms actually operate in construction. For example, instead of general profit-maximizing behaviour from standard economic theory, construction firms often focus on short-term cost reduction in order to complete projects profitably. In order to survive, firms need to ensure not only that they are profitable but also that they can anticipate their cash flow requirements. An important priority for the managers of any firm, and especially in construction, is therefore the management of cash flow and working capital.

In construction, marginal costs include the additional cost of utilizing the fixed capital assets needed to produce the extra unit of output as well as marginal prime costs. The marginal prime costs are the direct costs of supplying the extra work needed to produce the extra unit of output and may include labour, materials and the hiring of tools and plant. In any case, a building firm has little or no control over how much to produce and cannot change that quantity to suits its own purposes. This is because, in construction, output is concerned with projects, many of which are very large and entail the hiring or purchase of equipment that may go on to other projects after the current project ends. For example, construction product manufacturers, such as firms that supply domestic boilers, can use marginal cost pricing – that is, pricing based on the marginal cost – to determine the level of output for pricing their output. However, it is unusual for contractors to use this method, not least because it is extremely difficult to calculate in practice in the construction industry. Instead, contractors use mark-ups or full cost pricing to determine the tender prices they submit to clients.

Although this theoretical economic approach, called marginal cost pricing, explains the derivation of the profit-maximizing level of output, it does not determine the quantity to produce as far as construction contractors are concerned. Contractors rarely have the luxury of choosing the quantity they produce, apart from deciding whether or not to bid for projects as and when they come to the market.

Instead, precise output quantity decisions are taken by developers and planners, who, during the planning and design stages, negotiate between themselves and decide how much construction to build. The profits of contractors are not the concern of clients, planners and their advisors at this stage. Indeed, contractors repeatedly argue in favour of early involvement in projects, as it is then that their expertise can be used to improve designs and specifications. A building may be ten or 20 storeys tall, depending on planning permission; the design and shape of the building is often determined by the shape of the site and the surrounding buildings. The commercial interests of contractors, including the profitability and cost implications of building designs, are not usually considered at the early stages of projects, often because they have not yet been appointed. However, with the increasing use of building information modelling (BIM) and information technology (IT), changes in technology may well drive changes in the practices of construction clients and their contractors in the future. It is quite possible that, in future, contractors will need to become involved at the pre-construction stages of projects as they participate in integrated project management, which brings firms together to cooperate on design and planning the construction in order to avoid problems arising on site, such as clashes when two independent components or systems compete for the same space in the building. Nevertheless, it is still common for contractors to manage their businesses using full cost pricing, which is discussed in the next section.

The theory of marginal cost pricing assumes that owners of firms are in a position to decide exactly how much to produce in order to maximize their profits. They would still have to take into account whether or not they could sell all their profit-maximizing level of output or whether they would have to adjust their production downwards and forgo some profit. This is the standard account of maximizing profits in economics when firms control their own output levels.

However, often in construction it is the clients who decide the level of output, acting in their own interest and not in the best interest of the contractors.

After all, why should they? Clients are influenced by planning constraints, and not the maximum profits of contractors. The size of buildings, and hence the quantity contractors produce, is not decided by the contractors. This puts the contractors at a distinct disadvantage compared to firms in other industries. Most theories of production do not take into account the economic circumstances of firms in the construction industry. More recently, de Valence (2015) points to lean construction as the only theory of production targeted at the construction industry.

Lean construction has been adapted from lean production or lean manufacturing, borrowed from practice in other industries such as the automobile industry. According to Koskela (1997), lean manufacturing rests on the idea that, in manufacturing, only the transformation of materials into finished goods adds value. Lean production relies on a number of principles, including reducing non-value-adding activities, reducing production cycle times (the time from when materials enter the place of production until they depart) and simplifying production by reducing the steps that need to be taken in manufacturing a product or the number of separate components that need to be handled. The management techniques adopted by lean construction include just in time (JIT) and total quality management (TQM). JIT coordinates inward and outward deliveries to arrive and depart as and when needed, reducing waiting times and the need to hold stock. For example, car firms may hold only as little as one hour's worth of stocks in reserve, relying on deliveries to arrive on time, when needed. The objectives of TQM are to eliminate errors and remove the need to redo work.

The economics of the construction industry is distinct from manufacturing, in which the output often consists of identical or standardized products manufactured in production runs. In construction, every building project has unique characteristics, including the nature of the site, the type of building, the design of the building and the requirements of the client. The unique nature of every building project determines the business model that contractors have to adopt in order to survive. It determines the way in which construction firms operate. The construction industry business model therefore focuses on adaptability and flexibility.

It should be noted that the focus has primarily been on build to order, in which the client determines what is built. With developers building for speculative purposes, such as house building, there are opportunities to determine

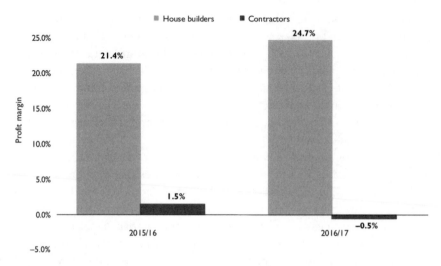

Figure 3.1 Profit margins of the top ten UK house builders and building contractors (2015/16 & 2016/17)
Source: London Stock Exchange

the quantity that they wish to produce and to determine the price on the basis of their estimates of marginal costs and the marginal revenue, based on demand from the consumer. Furthermore, they are able to determine and apply a mark-up that reflects demand in the general housing market. As a consequence, profit margins for speculative demand construction, such as for large house builders, are consistently considerably higher than for large building contractors in general, illustrated in Figure 3.1. In 2015/16 the average margin of the top ten UK house builders was 21.4 per cent, compared to an average margin of only 1.5 per cent for the top ten UK building contractors. Likewise, in 2016/17, whereas the average margin for the top ten UK house builders rose to 24.7 per cent, the average margin of the top ten UK building contractors fell to −0.5 per cent.

Tendering and full cost pricing in build to order

The quantity that contractors build is determined by the contracts they win, usually by tendering or bidding for the work in competition with other builders. Contractors compete in the market by tendering sequentially for work, usually one project at a time. The problem is that they do not know at the beginning of the year how busy they will be during the year as a whole. Not only do they have to estimate the construction cost of individual projects but they also need to allow for the share of total annual overhead costs that need to be spread across all projects depending on the size of each project. They therefore need to make assumptions about costs, turnover and profit margins. At the beginning of their financial year contractors do not know how many tenders they will win, how much they will be asked to build and the cost of labour, materials and plant hire needed to build it. Contractors therefore have to make their best estimate of their costs and how much of their overhead costs, including the cost of tendering, should be added to the total direct or prime cost of each tender bid as a mark-up, which also includes their own profit margin. As profit margins tend to be extremely low and small percentage differences can make the bid for work successful or unsuccessful, this makes the survival of contractors very precarious. For contractors, it is a matter of estimation and judgement, deciding how their existing workload (and contracts) meets the firm's capacity in the coming period. For this reason, contractors use a simple cost-plus pricing technique to estimate their tender bids.

Table 3.1 illustrates this method. The first stage is to estimate the prime or direct costs – for example, the quantity and levels of labour skills needed and what the rates of pay are likely to be. The types, quality and quantities of materials needed and the types and cost of hiring plant are included in a bill of quantities. All other costs are overhead costs or head office costs, including the staff needed to manage and administer the firm, such as a wages department, accounts department and an estimating department to submit tenders

Table 3.1 Cost-plus pricing in construction

Mark-up percentage covers:
Profits
Cost of finance
Head office costs
Contingencies and risk
Prime costs cover:
Labour
Materials
Tool and plant hire

for those projects the firm may not even win, which nevertheless must come out of the revenues from successful bids.

The bidding strategy must include a sufficient mark-up percentage of prime costs to cover the firm's costs of borrowing and its profit margin, although at the beginning of the financial year the firm cannot know how much work it will win and, therefore, how much of a profit margin to charge clients. Nevertheless, if it is tendering for work, it must estimate a share of the overhead costs to be borne by the first job tendered, assuming the firm will win some tender competitions later on in the year, based on an estimate of the firm's expectation of its total annual forthcoming sales revenues. Each project then represents a percentage of expected turnover. This may put contractors under pressure to win contracts later in the year to make up for the mark-ups at the beginning of the year, which assumed the firm would win further contracts later on.

An overestimate of the coming year's workload would lead the firm to charge too small a mark-up to clients at the beginning of the year and then have to make up the shortfall towards the end of the year to avoid making a loss on the year's trading. Adding high mark-ups towards the end of the year would make the firm's bids uncompetitive and unattractive to clients, making it impossible to make up for underestimating what was needed at the beginning of the year. At the same time, the mark-up must include an element for profit, as one of the firm's aims must be to generate profits from each project. Without profits at the end of the year the firm does not have the funds to invest in its future and grow through new additional skills, capital, entrepreneurship and management.

Firms may increase the likelihood of winning the vast majority of projects that they bid for, but this is likely only if they submit bids that have a low or negative margin. Contractors refer to this strategy as "leaving money on the table". This implies that contractors may have been able to submit higher tender prices for the work and still win the tender, although it should be noted that in a "blind" bidding process, in which contractors do not know what their competitors are bidding, the extent of the "money left on the table" on each potential contract is unknown.

Once the prime costs and the overhead costs have been estimated, a critically important factor still needs to be taken into account: the profit margin. The profit margin is the percentage profit mark-up, after all other costs have been taken into account. This profit margin has to take into account the need to reward the contractor for undertaking the work and compensating the firm for the risks it accepts as the builder. The profit element of the bid also needs to take into account the opportunity cost of taking on the project, instead of perhaps an alternative project that might have been more profitable or might have helped to establish contact with a client who had the potential to award more work to the contractor in the future and at a better profit margin – an opportunity that might be lost if only a narrow view was taken, to win every project, regardless of possible alternative clients who might also be interested in building at a higher profit margin for the contractor.

In spite of the difficulty of judging the correct or winning tender bid, contractors are aware of the competition, and their tender bids tend to be based on low profit margins of around 2 to 3 per cent, depending on their assessment of activity in the construction market (in addition to their need to win new contracts to utilize fixed cost factors of production and meet revenue targets). However, there can be exceptions to this rule, such as when a contractor has built up a relationship with the client through delivering a successful project in the past. Nevertheless, contractors' tender bids are usually very tight, leaving little room for error or negotiation, because it is assumed by all that the service provided by all contractors is identical, because the work and quality are specified in the tender documents and therefore the only difference between contractors is their tender price.

It is this low profit margin that is at the centre of understanding how the construction industry works. The low profit margins in contracting arise from the assumption that all contractors will build an identical product based on the client's specification and the only difference between contractors during the tendering process is the price they offer. Everything that occurs in construction relates back to the squeezed profits of contractors. Because the profit margins are so low, contractors cannot afford to make any concessions. For example, when a subcontractor incurs greater costs than expected, owing to delays, adverse weather conditions, the late arrival of materials or accidents on site, very often the subcontractor cannot be reimbursed for the extra costs incurred. As a result, disputes arise between main contractors and their specialist subcontractors, leading to distrust and a hostile and litigious industry, and further delays on site.

As a result of the competitiveness of the construction market and the assumed homogeneity of the construction services on offer as defined in the client's specification, profit margins in construction are usually extremely low. The profit margin is the profit over sales expressed as a percentage. When one considers the high value of projects and the great risks and uncertainties of building work, it is remarkable that firms are prepared to undertake the work in the first place. Competition in construction is tight, and a one- or two-percentage-point error can make the difference between winning a tender competition or not. The winning tender bid also depends on how keen competitors are to be awarded the contract. For example, if the construction market is buoyant and firms have a strong pipeline of projects, then competitors may charge a higher mark-up and price than they would have done if they had been anxious to win or if they felt threatened by the level of competition and were under pressure to win new contracts during a period with low or falling construction demand. In any case, winning a tender competition is not always profitable, because of the small margin of error allowed for with a low margin in the price agreed and the terms of the contract.

This is all the more pressing as all the contractors in a tender competition require very similar materials, specialist contractors, plant and labour. It is unlikely that prime costs will vary significantly between the competing contractors. The only significant difference between them is the mark-up they add to their prime costs, and this will depend on their need to win work to maintain their work load and their cash flow. Firms often survive by having cash payments from a number of different projects in the same period, which enables them to make payments even when payments on any one project might be delayed for any number of reasons, not necessarily the fault of the contractor. Alternatively, firms may resort to delaying payments to their sub-contractors or suppliers in order to maintain a positive cash flow.

During recessions, when construction demand is low, contractors may be so keen or desperate to win work at any price that they may not add a mark-up at all to the total construction costs submitted by their suppliers and sub-contractors. Instead, they may calculate the total direct or prime costs and then deduct a small percentage, in effect bidding a negative mark-up. This is sometimes called "buying in" work for the sake of having a cash flow to show the firm is still operating. Because of the lack of work, main contractors are aware that the prices of materials and hiring specialist contractors are also likely to go down in the near future. This expected reduction in construction costs is used by main contractors after they have won a tender competition to force their materials suppliers and specialist subcontractors to reduce their prices in order to remain in work on the project. The argument used is that the suppliers or subcontractors submitted their prices to the main contractor earlier in the tendering process to enable the main contractor to calculate the initial estimate of the total cost of the tender bid. Having won the tender competition, the main contractor is then in a stronger position to ask sub-contractors and suppliers to reduce their prices, with the work now certain. When this occurs it is known as a Dutch auction, which is disliked by specialist contractors. Main contractors persuade their subcontractors to reduce their prices by threatening them with replacement. Having been awarded the contract, the main contractor is now in a powerful position, increasing its negotiating strength relative to its suppliers and forcing them to reduce their prices. Although such strategies are unpopular, they reflect market conditions in the construction industry, especially when supply is greater than demand.

Nevertheless, market dynamics mean that construction prices are constantly in a state of flux. They may rise or fall as a result of changing input prices, such as wages, energy costs and materials, changing competitor prices and changing demand. For example, increases in construction demand may put pressure on firms' resources, making it more expensive to hire labour, or on another occasion a reduction in demand may create spare capacity and a downward pressure on prices throughout the supply chain. Other factors beyond the construction market may also influence demand, including cost inflation and interest rate changes, used by central banks, such as the Bank of England, to control inflation by raising the rate of interest to slow demand in the economy and reduce inflationary pressure.

A digression into accounting practice

Having described the general behaviour of construction firms in the market, it is time to take a closer look at what actually happens in terms of the internal management of accounts and cash flow. At any one time main contractors are, in effect, portfolios of projects. In other words, they may be engaged in building five or six separate projects. Together, these projects make up the workload of the firm. Some projects may be nearing completion while others are just beginning. Large firms tend to concentrate on large projects while smaller firms undertake the smaller schemes. Main contractors tend to concentrate on larger projects and subcontract out the work to specialist firms.

On the other hand, subcontractors may work on only one or two projects at a time, and are therefore vulnerable to cash flow problems if they are not paid on time, making them dependent on the main contractor.

Because of the difficulty of simultaneously managing projects, firms tend to keep the number of projects at any one time within a manageable span of control. The largest firms therefore tend to have a number of independent regional units or subsidiaries, all under the central control of the main board, but able to develop a regional identity and presence in order to make contact with potential clients and participate in tendering for work. These regional units are often the result of takeovers or mergers of regional firms by one of the larger construction firms. Such acquisitions have the advantage that the staff have local knowledge, contacts and marketing advantages, making it easier for a large contractor to take over the reputation of the local firm and develop it further.

Meanwhile, financial management is based on balance sheets and profit and loss accounts. The balance sheet measures the stock of wealth at a particular moment in time, while the profit and loss account measures the flows of receipts from sales and expenditures for purchases over a period, usually a year. The firm's stock of wealth increases if the flow of revenues is greater than the flow of expenditure. Sales or revenues represent inflows of money while purchases or expenditures represent outflows.

In the profit and loss account costs are deducted from sales revenues in stages (as shown in Table 3.2). Each stage indicates a meaningful and useful measure of profits and performance and conveys vital information for decision-makers, depending on the particular question asked. For example, what is the profit from trade? What is the underlying health of the firm before taking the burden of its debt into account? How much profit has the company generated after all deductions, including interest on past loans and tax?

The cost of sales is the direct cost of materials, labour and plant hire used in the production process. Direct costs are usually all costs associated with work on site, namely labour, materials and plant hire. Direct costs are the cost of sales, and direct costs are deducted from sales to calculate the gross profit,

Table 3.2 Definitions of the concepts used in the profit and loss account

Sales – revenues from sales

Other revenues – from sources of income other than sales, such as rent from properties owned

less cost of sales – direct costs for materials, labour and other costs such as design costs

equals gross profit – the difference between revenues and direct costs

less overhead costs – head office costs including rent, interest on loans, training costs, insurance

equals profits or earnings before interest and tax (EBIT)

less interest

equals profit before tax

less tax

equals net profits

so called because nothing has been deducted from sales apart from the direct costs of producing them. Gross profits show how much the core activity of the firm itself generates financially, out of which all expenses and overheads must eventually be paid.

Overhead costs are the costs associated with all aspects of running a company apart from the actual production function itself. Contractors may identify these overhead activities according to departmental headings, including the estimating department, the human resources or wages department, the marketing department, the research and development department (if there is one) and the accounts department. The cost of these overheads is deducted from gross profits to show earnings before interest and tax (EBIT). This is perhaps the most revealing measure of profits, as it takes into account not only how well the projects have been managed but also how effective management is at keeping administration costs under control and in line with the size of output. EBIT is, therefore, a good indicator of the performance of the firm under its current management. For example, EBIT does not take into account the debt burden of a firm, which can reduce the returns to shareholders, because of loans taken out by a previous management, through no fault of the current board.

Finally, of interest to shareholders but no less important than the other measures of profit is the profit after tax, or net profit. This shows the returns owned by the shareholders and gives the rate of return on the capital invested in the firm. Net profit over capital employed shows the rate of return, in the same way as the interest earned on the money deposited in a bank. This rate of return enables potential shareholders to measure the performance (and risk) of one firm compared to another. The return on capital employed is a major influence on the share price of firms, although it is not the only influence. Expectations of future performance also influence share prices, and these may have little to do with the actual performance of the firm itself. For example, changes in politics and the national economy may influence confidence in a company's ability to trade profitably in the future, adversely affecting its share price outside the control of the directors of the firm itself.

In terms of formal legal relationships, shareholders own construction companies, and hence the net profits belong to the shareholders too. In practice, some of the net profits may be distributed to shareholders and some retained by the firm, for future investment or to add to working capital, which is discussed below. The gross profit is the profit of each project before overheads have been deducted. The gross profit of each project measures the amount each project contributes towards the running of the company and the firm's profits. The grand total of the contributions of all its construction projects is the gross profit in the firm's profit and loss account.

Overhead costs are sometimes referred to as running costs, head office costs or on-costs, and these are not necessarily directly associated with any one particular project. Subtracting the overhead or indirect costs from gross profits gives earnings before interest and tax. EBIT is a clear measurement of the performance of the firm, showing how well the firm runs its projects and controls its overhead costs and cash flow, especially when EBIT is shown as a percentage of sales. By using the ratio of EBIT over sales, it is possible to assess whether a firm is improving its managerial efficiency, by showing how its profits are growing over time relative to sales.

Moving down the hierarchy of measures of performance in Table 3.2, interest payments are a tax-deductible expense, like any other costs that firms must pay. In other words, interest payments are deducted from profits before calculating the tax due on profits. Net profits after tax can either be retained in the firm or distributed to shareholders. The profit of each project is the difference between the revenue earned and the cost of producing the building or service. The net profit margin of a project is the profit after tax, expressed as a percentage of sales.

Apart from the difficulties of running projects, the challenge at the heart of managing a construction company itself is that the net profit margin is extremely low. This low profit margin is at the heart of operating a construction firm. There is no room for error or negotiation with suppliers and sub-contractors when delays occur or progress does not go according to plan, which is all too common in construction. A simple example will demonstrate the point.

A contractor is due to receive £100 million for completing a building according to the contract and the cost of the construction work including tax is £98 million, leaving the main contractor with a net profit of £2 million. The net profit margin is therefore 2/100, or 2 per cent. When profits are so low compared to the cost of construction, it takes only a small unexpected delay or addition to costs to eliminate the profit altogether. Indeed, there is a constant and high risk of a small profit turning into a loss. Every contract is both an opportunity to make a profit and a threat to the very survival of the firm. Making a profit that is only a small percentage of the value of each project means that a loss on one project can turn the profits generated from all other projects in a company's portfolio of contracts into a loss overall for the company. It is not unusual for firms to run into cash flow difficulties when there are insufficient cash reserves to make payments before receiving payments (possibly from other projects) due to the firm.

It is extremely difficult to convince banks and investors that the firm can turn the situation around once it is in financial trouble, because of the low profit margin and the time and work needed to revive the firm's financial state of health.

Low profit margins, cash flow and working capital are vital to understanding the pressures firms are under. The problem with working capital is that, in order to survive, a firm needs to be able to pay its labour costs, plant hire, materials and other bills, such as energy and head office costs, including rent and head office staff, as well as interest on bank borrowing or finance. All these costs need to be met, often before payment for work has been received. If there is insufficient cash held in reserve, otherwise known as working capital, and the firm cannot honour its debt obligations, then it is very likely that it will be forced to cease trading, even though it may have a number of projects in the pipeline, unless some arrangement with creditors can be found. Mostly, firms that experience cash flow difficulties do not survive, because banks and lenders lose confidence in a firm's ability to meet its debts. Lending more money to such a firm is likely to fail to save it, as cash flow difficulties are seen as a management failure, and in such a situation lending to or investing in a firm under those circumstances is seen as taking a high risk with weak management.

When profit margins are low, contractors cannot afford to employ labour except on a casual basis when it is needed on site. Unless building workers are working productively, adding value that generates income, any time spent not generating revenues becomes prohibitively expensive for firms and soon consumes what little in the way of cash reserves there may be. If, for example, profit margins are 2 per cent, then, for every £10 spent by the firm on unproductive labour, it needs to build and sell work worth £500, because £10 is 2 per cent of £500, the net profit of producing £500 worth of building work (see Equation 3.1). Otherwise, the firm does not generate enough revenue to cover the expense. Only a small proportion of the revenue is left after all other costs have been met. In profits, £10 is 2 per cent of £500 of turnover:

$$£10 \times 100/2 = £500 \qquad \text{Equation 3.1}$$

However, at a profit margin of 4 per cent, the contractor needs to sell only £250 of work to cover the £10 of unproductive labour:

$$£10 \times 100/4 = £250 \qquad \text{Equation 3.2}$$

The greater the profit margin, the less revenue a firm needs to generate for a given expenditure and the more room it has to make concessions with its supply chain and employers. However, the small profit margins found in the construction industry mean that it is not surprising that contractors are parsimonious when it comes to taking on permanent staff and site labour and training them, or, indeed, incurring any kind of expense or committing to any non-essential risk. In construction when projects are discrete, distinct or separate from other projects, projects may come to an end before more work is available, even when firms have several projects running at the same time. Once again, an issue arises in construction when continuity of work for site labour is constrained because of the low profit margins. Specialist staff, for example, may not be required once a project comes to an end. Utilizing and switching trades across different projects smoothly and without a gap is not always possible and is not usually practical or achievable.

Construction firms can easily run into cash flow difficulties, taking firms by surprise, especially when they are busy and growing rapidly. Indeed, it is often the rapid expansion of a firm that leads to cash flow problems arising in the first place. As contractors have little direct control over the volume of work they undertake, for reasons discussed earlier, firms can find themselves undertaking far larger projects than they might have anticipated, especially when unanticipated problems arise on site, and payments to the contractor are delayed or withheld.

As far as the contractor is concerned, many payments cannot be postponed. Punctuality with interest payments, for example, is essential. Otherwise, the bank could constrain further lending needed by the contractor, or, in the worst circumstances, foreclose on the loan facility, demanding the whole amount of the loan be repaid immediately. Rent, too, must be covered, or the firm could risk eviction from its premises. If wages are not paid in full, workers may walk off the site, stopping construction work and all progress, cutting the firm off from its cash flow and main source of future revenue. Managing cash flow involves understanding working capital.

The operating cycle and the current ratio

Working capital (WC) is the cash, bank accounts or shares held in other companies that a firm can call on to meet its day-to-day expenditure on wages, interest payments for past borrowing and other items that enable the firm to continue functioning. Also included in working capital is cash borrowed or held in the form of an overdraft facility, which enables the firm to borrow, if and when required. If the cash available dwindles towards zero, the firm simply cannot continue to trade, and hence managing cash flow is central to a firm's survival.

The flows of cash into contractors take the form of interim payments from the employers of projects the contractor has been commissioned to build. Outflows of cash take the form of payments for material supplies, interest payments, rent and wages. If payments to the firm are delayed, the firm must still be able to pay its suppliers, its workforce and other binding financial obligations. The amount of money needed depends on the length of the credit period suppliers are willing to wait for payment and the length of time debtors take to settle their accounts with the firm.

In accountancy terms, working capital is equivalent to net current assets. Net current assets are current assets less current liabilities.

$$WC = \text{current assets} - \text{current liabilities} \qquad \text{Equation 3.3}$$

Current assets are comprised of cash held, the value of work done but not yet paid, and materials held in stock that can readily be turned into cash, if necessary. Current liabilities are the payments due to be paid in the short term, usually before the end of the current financial year. Working capital also includes the total value of cash owed to the firm by its trade debtors less money it owes its trade creditors. A guide to the amount of working capital required is the ratio of working capital to turnover. This can be measured as a percentage of the turnover from previous years' accounts. This relates the working capital to the size of the firm's operations, as shown in Equation 3.4.

$$WCR = WC/TO \times 100 \qquad \text{Equation 3.4}$$

where

WCR = working capital requirement
WC = working capital
TO = turnover

In practice, WC amounts to current assets including cash reserves and loan facilities less current liabilities less current bank loans.

Current assets may take the form of stocks and materials, and converting these into cash for payments might not be achieved quickly enough to meet the needs of creditors. Excluding stocks and materials from current assets may therefore provide a more relevant measure of current assets, closer to what accountants call the acid test.

Table 3.3 presents an alternative approach to measuring the need for working capital based on the operating cycle, which is the average length of time between the inward delivery of materials and payment for the work.

Table 3.3 The operating cycle

Operation	Weeks
Average time between delivery of materials and application on site	2
less builders' merchants' credit period	4
Residual of builders' merchants' credit period	−2
plus average time taken to use materials on site	3
plus average time between production and certification	3
plus average time taken by debtors to settle accounts	11
Total operating cycle	15

As an example, Table 3.3 shows how an operating cycle can be used to calculate the size of working capital required when the total operating cycle is 15 weeks. Given that working capital is needed to bridge a 15-week gap in cash flow, then, if the annual turnover or value of sales is £1 million, the WCR is 15/52 multiplied by £1 million – equal to £288,462, or approximately a quarter of turnover.

If the firm had been able to cut its operating cycle to eight weeks, the working capital required would have been reduced to 8/52 × £1 million, or £153,846, which is approximately a sixth of the cost of sales. The shorter the operating cycle, the lower the working capital requirement.

The WCR depends on both the length of the operating cycle and the size of annual turnover. The WCR is even more important when a firm is experiencing rapid growth, which often occurs in construction when SMEs are awarded larger contracts than they are able to manage financially. As firms expand, reference to past performance is not necessarily useful, as the working capital is needed to accommodate *additional* costs and a widening working capital gap *in the future*. In an expanding firm, the percentage of capital that is needed to be set aside for WC is even greater than the ratios indicated above would imply, where the firm is not necessarily growing.

WC is the amount needed to oil the wheels of the firm to enable it to continue trading. One method of influencing the amount of working capital needed is to delay payments to suppliers, while insisting on prompt payment from customers. For instance, the British contractor Carillion paid many sub-contractors only after 126 days. Consequently, this reduced Carillion's working capital cash requirement and exploited the free loan periods of credit to their own advantage.

Being aware of the operating cycle of a firm enables the amount needed for working capital to be estimated on the basis of future turnover rather than any historical ratio. This matters if cash flow difficulties are to be avoided, as the firm needs to know how well it manages its cash flow by using the debtor days (the average number of days it gives its customers to pay) and creditor days (the average number of days it takes to pay its creditors). Shortening the debtor days and lengthening the creditor days reduces the amount of working capital needed by using cash flow to delay payments to suppliers and speeding up payments due from clients.

Number of debtor days = debtors/credit sales for the year × 365

Equation 3.5

Equation 3.5 gives an estimate of the average number of days it takes the firm to receive money from sales. The average number of days the firm takes to pay its suppliers and subcontractors is given in Equation 3.6.

Number of creditor days = creditors/cost of sales × 365   Equation 3.6

A positive cash flow increases a firm's liquidity, the amount of cash at its disposal. A negative cash flow occurs when firms owe more than they receive in revenues. This is often deliberately managed in construction, where contractors use the money they owe to suppliers by deliberately delaying payments in order to stretch the period of their credit days at the expense of their suppliers, but this is a high-risk strategy for many contractors and not necessarily desirable in terms of the firm's reputation.

Cash flow may be used to plan the timing of payments and measure the financial capacity of the firm to take on risk. Knowing when payments are due has been used by main contractors to time the payments to subcontractors by using "pay when paid" clauses, although they were always frowned upon by subcontractors and are often the cause of disputes within the construction team. Officially, "pay when paid" clauses are no longer legally accepted. However, Gruneberg and Murdoch (2011) point out that surveys of subcontractors have regularly highlighted that such payment practices continue to be frequently delayed and adversely affect cash flow. These delays in payment often form a constraint on the ability of firms to expand or take on more work.

Cash flow and working capital are major constraints on the rate of growth. When firms expand, the increased turnover requires additional working capital so as to meet the need to pay greater expenses prior to firms being paid by their customers. It is, therefore, essential for the survival of the firm that contractors always have sufficient cash in reserve to pay their creditors, staff, interest and taxes, although in practice this is not always possible. Indeed, failure to take cash flow into account can lead to the demise of a firm even when it is busy and growing. Firms need working capital in order to survive.

An example of the operating cycle, cash flow and working capital

The operating cycle is the average length of time from the start of the building process until payments are received. Production begins with the delivery of materials. These may remain unused, on average for a short period of time, before they are incorporated into the building process. Fortunately, this delay can be offset if material suppliers offer a period of credit, usually up to one month. However, production takes time, and payments to suppliers may become due before interim payments become due from the client. Moreover, interim payments may be delayed because of certification issues, if there are problems satisfying the architect or surveyor and work is not signed off. Even after certificates have been issued, clients may delay payments.

If the average time taken from the delivery of materials to final payment is eight weeks, then the minimum working capital requirement is 8/52 of the firm's annual turnover. If the firm's turnover is £10 million per year, then the working capital required is £10 million multiplied by 8/52, which is equivalent to £1.5 million. However, if the payments are delayed by a further eight weeks on average, then the working capital requirement increases to 16/52 of expected turnover, namely £3.1 million, an increase of cash reserves of £1.5 million. Each additional week of the operating cycle would require an additional £192,000 (1/52 × £10 million). In other words, in order to establish a buffer in the firm's financial structure, even short delays may end up being extremely costly for suppliers, who are waiting for their payments.

Of course, retention payments form only a small proportion of a firm's total revenues. Nevertheless, for a firm with a turnover of £10 million and a production cycle of eight weeks, assuming its retention payments amounted to 5 per cent of turnover, as reported by Hughes, Hillebrandt and Murdoch (2000), an average delay of only one week in receiving its retention payments would result in an increase of £86,500 in the firm's working capital requirement. However, delays in retention payments are generally considerably longer than one week. This represents non-productive capital as far as the contractor is concerned. Nevertheless, it is essential for the firm to set cash aside for working capital in order for it to survive. This working capital is the firm's own capital but it cannot be used by the contractor, because the cash is needed to meet its current liabilities, as a result of delays in retention payments extending the production cycle.

Because firms in the construction industry tend to have a relatively small portfolio of projects, each project constitutes a high percentage of turnover. As this feature is combined with low profit margins, one of the challenges firms face is that each project represents both an opportunity to make a significant improvement to the profits of the firm and, at the same time, a threat. As a result, if a firm is not paid or is not paid for one of its projects within a short period of time, it may incur critical cash flow difficulties affecting the very survival of the firm itself, with consequences for its other projects and its subcontractors and suppliers, who may be waiting for payments for work already carried out.

In the example of the firm with a turnover of £10 million, let us assume a retention payment is withheld on a project worth £1 million. The impact of this on the cash flow is 5 per cent of £1 million, which amounts to £50,000. If this payment is withheld for one year, the firm must find £50,000 in the short term to bridge its financial cash flow difficulties. Even if the payment is forthcoming after six months, the amount of funding needed to replace the hole in its cash flow in those six months is still £25,000. The worst scenario occurs when firms go out of business while owing retention money to their suppliers, even though the work carried out by suppliers in good faith may even have been certified. In these cases retention payments are rarely forthcoming.

As we have seen, firms in the construction industry often work on profit margins as low as 2 per cent of turnover, so £50,000 represents the profits from £2,500,000 worth of turnover. In other words, to be able to afford the loss or delay of a payment amounting to £50,000, this firm would need to spend the gains from 25 per cent of its total turnover to cover the cost of a serious delay in its retention payment in one of its projects. In terms of working capital planning over the longer term, the working capital requirement would be an additional £50,000 if payment was withheld for one year or £25,000 if it was withheld for only six months. If the percentage of turnover of one project were even greater, this cash flow difficulty would be exacerbated.

One of the root causes of these cash flow difficulties is the low profit margins in the construction industry. If profit margins were closer to 10 per cent, firms could accumulate reserves more quickly and survive for longer when there were delays in receiving payments from customers.

Somehow contractors have to navigate their way through a complex set of market arrangements, which occasionally fails as a consequence of ferocious competition and the willingness to take on cash flow risk and the risk of making a loss on a project. The case study below illustrates the consequences of the combination of low profit margins, subcontracting and the difficulties of managing the uncertainties of the construction process.

CASE STUDY 1: CARILLION

The business model of main contractors primarily focuses on winning projects and managing them, with the activity and risk subcontracted out to the supply chain. However, the incentives this creates in focusing on boosting revenue and optimistic accounting for short-term gain pose key risks to the main contractor itself and all the firms in its construction supply chain. This was highlighted in the collapse of Carillion in 2018.

Carillion, the UK's second largest contractor, was liquidated on 15 January 2018. It had 19,500 employees across 326 companies and accounted for £5.2 billion in total revenue in 2016 across all its operations, over a half of which were in public sector support services. Carillion's UK construction arm had 199 registered companies and a total revenue of £1.5 billion in 2016 coming from its UK construction activity.

At the point of its demise there were 72 key construction projects on which Carillion was working, spread primarily across the infrastructure and commercial sectors but also with projects in the defence, education and health sectors. Large construction programmes involve a great amount of resourcing and a high degree of risk. Estimating time and cost on large, bespoke projects that often take years is particularly difficult given the number of factors that can change in cost, whether it be finance, labour/skills, plant and machinery, tools, the extent of rework if something is done incorrectly and changes in the specification of a bespoke project during the project itself.

As a major contractor, Carillion focused on minimizing the risk, often operating in joint ventures with other main contractors on the large projects and subcontracted work. In addition, it also hired plant and tools/machinery rather than owning them, a common practice in UK construction. As a consequence, the key impacts of the Carillion liquidation will be on the firms reliant on it for work, the direct subcontractors and suppliers.

In addition to employing 19,500 people, it also had 11,687 direct subcontractors and suppliers, according to the Department for Business, Energy and Industrial Strategy. These subcontractors and suppliers also had subcontractors and suppliers, which means that, in total, an estimated 25,000 to 30,000 subcontractors and suppliers were affected by the liquidation of Carillion.

As the majority of the activity was subcontracted out, Carillion's main activity was primarily winning and managing contracts. A key problem with this business model is that the incentive is then to win as many projects as possible across as many different areas as possible, even at low margins, which, given the difficulty regarding estimating costs on projects that have still to be built, may become negative margins when costs rise. To deal with issues around profitability, Carillion pushed the problems down the supply chain, and its standard terms were to pay subcontractors only 126 days after the work had been done; the company moved to these terms of business in 2013, which gave Carillion time to profit from the difference between when it was paid and when it had to pay the supply chain for activity.

Furthermore, Carillion instituted an early repayment facility, in which subcontractors could be paid in 45 days but would have to pay Carillion for the privilege. Carillion also used retentions, whereby the major contractor keeps a proportion of the fee charged by subcontractors for the construction work. The intervals between receiving the income and paying the supply chain and the retentions effectively become areas for margin or additions to profit for the major contractor. However, the subcontractors are the part of the supply chain least able to deal with later or delayed payment, paying to receive payment for work on time and receiving less of the retention after the work. In the construction sector subcontractors are the most reliant on cash flow to survive and have the least access to additional finance if they need it.

In addition, the incentive for the major contractor is to find other areas in which the value of the company can be boosted in the company's accounts. For instance, in its final full year of financial reporting, the firm's largest asset was goodwill. Goodwill is the company's own valuation of intangible assets, assets that are not visible, and, as a consequence, it is very difficult to measure. It includes the value of the Carillion brand, relations with clients, the benefits of activity other than contracts (such as sporting sponsorship) and potential backlogs in orders. At the end of 2016 Carillion stated that the value of its goodwill was £1.6 billion, an amount greater than its UK construction turnover in that year.

It is possible to draw conclusions from this management behaviour. Major contractors were also able to boost the company's value in its most recent financial accounts prior to Carillion's final collapse by optimistically assuming that revenue on projects would occur early. For instance, £294 million of Carillion's revenue in December 2016 was traded but not yet certified, which meant that it had not been signed off by the client. However, this implied that it was a risky strategy for contractors, because it meant that they were subject to serious financial issues, if there were serious conflicts with the client regarding the quality of the work. In Carillion's case, it won a contract in 2011 with Msheireb Properties, a Qatari company, to develop a mixed-use scheme that was due to complete in 2014 but remained incomplete in 2018, with both the client and Carillion in conflict arguing that each owed the other £200 million.

Another method of boosting revenue to make the major contractor appear to be in good financial health is to purchase other firms, which Carillion did across many different areas. This tactic boosts total revenue and market capitalization on the stock exchange. In addition, theoretically, it also means that the firm diversifies its risk across different areas. However, this also dilutes core activities and ends up with diseconomies of scale, whereby two firms together often underperform the aggregation of the individual firms. Such mergers or takeovers may just add to the complexity and the bureaucracy, which exacerbates losses when the company is in difficulties or the sector is in trouble.

In 2017 Carillion was forced to write down the value of construction projects by £1.2 billion, primarily as a consequence of losses on just four projects. Given its UK construction turnover of £1.5 billion, the level of write-downs was unsustainable. Furthermore, at the point of its demise in January 2018, its debt was £900 million, with a pension deficit of £590 million, and it had cash reserves of only £28 million. Given that its construction activity was primarily subcontracted out, Carillion had few assets, and, as a consequence, it went straight into liquidation, rather than (as is general practice for large firms in the UK) going into administration, agreeing a deal with creditors to reduce debt and restructuring operations before continuing as a firm going forward. Carillion illustrates an extreme case, and the particular business model was unsustainable in the long term. Nevertheless, many of the practices undertaken by Carillion are also undertaken by other main contractors.

Concluding remarks

One of the main points of this chapter has been to show how contractors operate in the construction market in contrast with the economic principles that inform general economic theory in most sectors of the economy. In manufacturing, for example, firms need to calculate the marginal cost and the marginal revenue, in order to find out how much to produce and how much to charge. The price they wish to charge is then compared to the prices offered by their competitors.

This contrasts with what occurs in construction, in which contractors bid for work in auctions. The lowest bid usually wins. This has the effect of reducing the percentage mark-up contractors add to the cost of their suppliers, their subcontractors, for fear of losing the opportunity of winning the opportunity to take on the project, because their percentage mark-up was too high. Having won the work for a fixed price, the contractors then have to work out how they might increase their profit margin by finding ways of reducing their costs in the course of carrying out the work. This leads to many disagreements, which often end up in court.

Because the profit margins in construction tend to be very low, firms have little opportunity for negotiation. For this reason, the construction industry is often seen as litigious. Contractors are aware that, if they lose money on a project, they have to take on a lot of work to make up for the shortfall. As a result, contractors avoid risks if they can, engage labour only if there is work available and rarely invest in plant and machinery. Instead, they hire it.

4

THE FIRM AND ECONOMIES OF GROWTH

This chapter explains how economies (or savings) of growth are the drivers of expansion, as growth enables firms to remain competitive. This relentless pressure to expand has existed since the rise of capitalist production replaced feudal methods.

In the eighteenth century, before the Industrial Revolution, construction markets in Britain were regulated by guilds of master craftsmen. The guilds controlled each trade, prices and quality. They also controlled the number of journeymen and apprentices who could be employed by each master craftsman. This limited the ability of any one master to gain power over his competitors. However, from approximately the 1750s to the 1820s, the Industrial Revolution and the Napoleonic Wars did much to undermine the power of the guilds, and gradually they were replaced by a market system.

Since then markets have remained competitive, favouring the most efficient firms and often the most ruthless. Ever since the arrival of the market in construction there has been pressure on firms to increase sales, increase profits and raise the productivity of staff on site and in contractors' offices to improve competitiveness. The ever-present pressure to increase sales implies the need to increase the size of the firm, as measured by the size of turnover, number of people employed, value of assets or some other yardstick. Under market conditions it has never been possible for firms to rest on their laurels, take it easy and relax.

How firms meet this challenge of continuous expansion is explained in this chapter. It is a challenge that has a price, as society today becomes increasingly aware of the limits to growth caused by environmental degradation, the non-sustainability of declining resources and pollution. Increasingly sustainability has become an issue in construction, and writers such as Kate Raworth (2017) point out that the economy is simply not able to expand its consumption of resources at its current rate and dump the resulting waste in the environment. Such writers describe an attitude towards the economy as a whole that questions the need to continue on a growth path indefinitely.

However, the moment a firm ceases to grow, it begins to fall behind at least some of its competitors. Firms pursue growth continuously by diversifying into new markets or products. According to the theory of company growth, firms invest in the latest plant and machinery, which embodies the latest technology. They train staff in the latest techniques and increase the numbers employed. To ensure they remain competitive, firms are under constant pressure from their rivals to invest in new plant and machinery, labour and skills, management and marketing.

In construction, investment in plant and machinery and training, as well as a number of other important areas such as digitalization, off-site manufacturing, management and entrepreneurship, is limited. One reason is that, apart from a few large contractors, low profit margins make it expensive and risky for contractors to commit to high up-front investments in plant that enables a long-term rate of return, as they may not use the plant sufficiently to justify the initial investment, and the cost of training for many small contractors makes it attractive for them to employ casual labour on a temporary basis, without the guarantee of permanent continuous employment. These are the consequences of the low profit margins in construction, as noted in the previous chapter.

However, in other markets, competitors are permanently watching the behaviour and performance of other firms in the market, looking out for weaknesses, gaps in the market and opportunities to expand at the expense of their weakest rivals. In general, if a firm does not invest, carry out research or develop competitive advantages as much as its competitors, then it will eventually cease to keep up with them. A competitive advantage is the offer a firm makes that embodies the benefits of dealing with it because of its superior technology, quality, service or product compared to its competitors. For example, expertise or the ownership of specialist plant and machinery can strengthen a firm's ability to provide a more attractive, less costly or speedier service or product than its competitors, and can increase its sales or profit margins as a result.

The full benefit of acquiring a competitive advantage may not be immediate, as it can take several years for investments to yield a return. Nevertheless, by investing in areas such as training, new plant and equipment and new methods of managing the construction process, firms can maintain or improve turnover, profit and returns to capital, and, by increasing the productivity of the workforce, they can pay higher wages without raising their prices. However, in construction plant is often hired when required on a project-by-project basis, and a considerable proportion of the labour and skills is not permanently employed but subcontracted out. As a result, firms do not compete on the technology that they can offer or the skills of their workforce, who are subcontracted for the duration of the project, or often just for their part of the project.

In many other industries, firms that lag behind in investment terms eventually lose their competitive advantage and become less productive, less competitive and less profitable compared to their rivals. The firm enters a downward spiral of lower profits followed by less investment, which is then followed by even lower profits. This decline results from the initial lack of profits, which are the ultimate source of funds for investment purposes. The firm uses its profits to pay interest to lenders and repay loans. The only other source of investment funding is when shareholders are prepared to sink capital into the firm to help it to invest in plant and machinery or to finance a project or undertake innovative new techniques. However, this is likely to occur only for a firm that is currently profitable or likely to be in the near term.

A reduction in profits implies that fewer funds are available for investment purposes in the future, compared to other firms. The ultimate source of investment funding is the profit generated from sales. If shareholders expect profits to decline, then a firm's share price will be adversely affected as potential shareholders are deterred from investing. If they see problems ahead, confidence in the firm evaporates. If its share price declines, the firm can become vulnerable to a takeover from a rival firm, or even be bought by an asset stripper or hedge fund. Asset strippers are investment companies that distinguish between the trade of the firm and the value of its assets. If assets can be sold off at a higher price than the capital worth of the capitalized value of its annual sales less costs, then the firm may be worth more stripped of its assets than it is as a trading entity.

The net sales are equivalent to the annual sales of the firm less all its expenses at an acceptable rate of return or rate of interest, or discount rate. For example, 5 per cent may be used to convert the annual net income to an equivalent capital value. Thus, if the net annual sales of a firm are £10 million, to find the equivalent capital value, we ask the question: what is £10 million 5 per cent of? The answer is £200 million. This is because 5 per cent of £200 million is £10 million. If the value of assets belonging to the firm is valued at £250 million, then the capital value of a firm is worth more if its assets are sold off than if it continues as a going concern.

In the construction industry, it is often the case that contractors fail to carry out investment because of low profit margins and low returns, which means that the risk associated with investment is prohibitive. Nevertheless, firms still need to grow in order to take advantage of economies of scale and the benefits of size.

In Chapter 2 we introduced the concept of average cost (AC), or the total cost per unit of output. The average cost curve is a U-shaped curve (see Figure 2.3). To begin with, at low levels of output, the AC, or cost per unit, declines. It then reaches a minimum point and begins to increase. At low output levels, as output increases, the cost per unit declines, by virtue of the fact that the scale of production has increased. The firm thus takes advantage of economies of scale, or savings of size. By increasing production, the firm is able to reduce the cost of each unit of output. Mass production is more efficient than bespoke production, as time and money can be saved when dealing with large numbers. For this reason, quantity discounts are usually offered by builders' merchants to encourage bulk buying, which reduces the cost of administration per unit bought and sold.

However, as output increases, the AC curve declines at first, reaches a minimum and then begins to increase. In this phase of the curve, increasing the quantity produced serves only to increase the cost per unit. This occurs because the pressure of work on a small firm leads to mistakes being made, work being rushed, overtime having to be paid and expensive delays perhaps occurring, as workers wait for instructions. When the AC is increasing with output, as the firm grows it incurs diseconomies of scale, making each unit more expensive to produce compared to its competitors. If a firm incurs diseconomies of scale it is operating at a higher level of output than is efficient. By reducing the quantity produced the firm lowers the cost of producing each unit of output. The most efficient level of output is the minimum point on the

AC curve. The definition of the most efficient level of output is that level of output which uses the fewest resources to produce each unit, as measured by the least cost, including labour, materials, plant and machinery, and all head office costs.

In the context of this chapter, economies of scale are important to bear in mind, because they are a source of competitiveness and help to generate income through mass production. However, economies of scale are quite distinct from economies of growth, which are the main focus of this chapter.

Why firms feel the need to grow

In the seminal book *The Theory of the Growth of the Firm*, first published in 1959, Edith Penrose considers the performance of individual firms and demonstrates that, as long as firms are growing, they are in a strong position to compete in the market. For example, as long as contractors were growing they would be able to compete with other contractors, but as soon as their rate of growth slowed down, or they stopped expanding altogether, their relative costs of production would rise and they would become less competitive compared to their rival contractors.

According to Penrose, firms invariably have some spare capacity, which by definition is idle. This occurs because production uses a variety of skills and equipment. Not all skills and resources are used or needed all the time. As a result, some employees and plant experience periods of idleness until they are required to work again. Nevertheless, these resources have to be paid even when they are not productively employed. Finding useful work for idle resources is, therefore, effectively costless to the firm, because the firm must pay for them whether they are utilized or not. However, the firm still has to pay for other additional resources required for production to take place, but it does not have to pay for the use of spare capacity as it is freely available.

Expanding the activities of the firm means that spare resources can be used to lower the marginal cost of the additional output compared to the firm's competitors. This reduction in the marginal cost of production gives the firm the opportunity to have a competitive advantage. In other words, by using up some of its spare capacity, a firm can produce more cheaply than rival firms, which need to pay additional costs for all the inputs they use. This gives the firm with spare capacity a competitive advantage, arising out of economies of growth.

According to Penrose (1959), assume a product is manufactured by company X, comprised of three distinct components, a, b and c, and each component is produced by a dedicated machine. As a result, a set of three machines, A, B and C, is needed to produce each of these components, respectively. However, each machine produces a different quantity of components per hour, because the parts vary in complexity. If type A machines can produce $3a$ components per hour, type B machines produce $4b$ per hour and type C machines $5c$ per hour and if only three units were manufactured, machine A would be fully utilized but the type B machine would be used only for 75 per cent of its full capacity and the type C machine would be used only for 60 per cent of its full capacity. The management question is: what level of output should be produced in order to keep all machines working at full capacity? To find the output that would keep all plant and labour fully occupied, the answer is found by using the lowest common multiple (LCM). In this example, the LCM is 60, and therefore the firm would need to produce 60 units of output. It would need 20 type A machines, 15 type B machines and 12 type C machines, and at an output of 60 units per hour all the machines would be fully utilized. However, there would be little point in producing 60 units if they could not all be sold. If demand were only for 30, 50 or 55 units, then spare capacity would mean some machines would still be unavoidably idle for a portion of the day and the firm would be in the same situation as before the expansion or diversification of production. Penrose calls these gaps in the use of plant and labour "interstices". While the firm may be propelled towards a growth path in order to be competitive, solving for one interstice can simply create new interstices, which gives the firm the opportunity for further expansion. This is one reason the firm is permanently on a growth trajectory. Nevertheless, in going for expansion, it is still vital to look at costs and revenues, as discussed in the previous chapter, to find out the implications for the profits of the firm. Although it is not the only objective of a company, it is most important for a firm to be profitable. Growth and efficiency are important, but they are of secondary importance compared to profits.

If, say, the level of demand required only 30 units per day, then only ten type A machines, each producing three components per day would be needed, and, similarly, eight type B machines each producing four components per day and six type C machines each producing five components per day. While type A and type C machines would be fully utilized in manufacturing 30 units, one of the eight type B machines would be required only for 50 per cent of the time, because seven type B machines would be working all the time to produce 28 components, but the eighth machine, although it had the capacity to make $4b$ components, has to make only two. For 50 per cent of the time it lies idle, and is a new interstice available to fuel further expansion of the firm. The challenge is to make the two surplus b components and find some profitable new use for them. In other words, the firm needs to expand again into new products or markets. The same principle applies to labour, when people with different skills have to be organized in such a way that enables them to be productive.

One option for the firm is to take advantage of interstices involving plant and labour and expand the operations of the firm by diversifying into new products or new markets. In this case, some of the production costs are avoided by absorbing spare capacity that would have been idle otherwise. If a factor of production is not being utilized, then making use of it has what economists call zero opportunity cost. The opportunity cost of using a production factor is not the direct cost of using it but the indirect loss that arises from losing out on a potential gain through using it for something else. However, if the factor of production is currently employed, then moving the resource to produce something else is at the expense of what might otherwise have been produced, and that production is then lost. An opportunity cost is the cost of an option in terms of the next best alternative. For example, if a developer has to decide which of two projects to build, either one in Liverpool or one in London, then the opportunity cost of the Liverpool project is the forgone profits of the London project, and the true cost of the Liverpool project is the forgone profits of the London project.

Idle spare capacity in firm X is unproductive. Anything that uses these unused resources is made at no opportunity cost to firm X, although of course production would still entail some costs, such as for materials and other labour or machine costs. We have seen that, by using spare capacity, firm X can produce a new product line or service for less than its competitors, assuming they would have to pay for all the resources used in the production process. The extra production therefore expands the output of the firm as it seeks to supply new markets and products using up its spare capacity. Such firms are in a strong position to remain competitive. This is the reason continuous investment in new capacity is also necessary to maintain a firm's competitive edge. Firms therefore need to grow in order to survive even though no single strategy on its own can guarantee survival and success.

A firm's growth may be measured using the change in the number of people employed, the value of assets, sales and market capitalization or aggregate share value, the total value of shares being a measure of the size of a firm. While the growth of the firm may be seen as essential for survival, according to many, including Penrose, not all researchers come to the same conclusion. For example, in their study of profitability and survival of firms in general, not necessarily in the construction industry, Delmar, McKelvie and Wennberg (2013) find that, at best, growth is weakly associated with profitability and survival. Yet they conclude that "profitability helps firms survive and grow". Penrose argues that high-quality managers are one of the scarcest resources of all. Their willingness to lead, to take risks and, most importantly, to innovate are also essential qualities needed for firms to grow.

Innovation in construction

Growth is often a consequence of innovation, which is the spread or adoption of new ideas, methods, materials, components or products. In construction, new products and processes are continuously being introduced on site by contractors and subcontractors. Apart from finding new construction components to produce, growth in sales in construction can be achieved if firms are able to diversify into new markets, services or products, especially when the resources at the disposal of the firm are versatile, adaptable or flexible. In the case of construction, diversification may mean moving into a new region and buying a firm already operating in the area. This immediately opens up access to new contacts with individuals and new business links to suppliers and potential clients, as well as gaining an established reputation for the acquiring company as a new entrant in the local market.

Nevertheless, the construction industry is often said to be reluctant to innovate. As change is constantly taking place, contractors have to adapt to new materials and methods. Construction products, for example, include materials, building components and construction plant and machinery. These markets are where invention and innovation take place on a daily

basis in construction, because, in the markets for materials and components, the profit margins tend to be higher and more sustainable than in
contracting firms, thus providing the funding needed for the investment
necessary for innovation in processes and products. In addition, as materials and products are more standardized than bespoke in on-site construction, materials and products are made in a manufacturing environment that
benefits from investment in capital, manufacturing management practices,
manufacturing entrepreneurship and skills. Moreover, in product markets
firms compete not just on price but also on the latest features included in
their products. These features are designed to make it easier and faster to
build, maintain or use less labour in the installation process. When these
features are pointed out to building firms in the course of marketing the
new products, they offer contractors an opportunity to cut costs and make
a small saving on the total cost of construction. This is always an attractive
proposition for contractors, because most contracts are based on a fixed
price and any savings, even in the short term, are a bonus for the contractor
or subcontractor. As a result, the profit margin on building components
tends to be higher than for contractors, as the price of building components
is based on their cash saving features and other benefits, whereas the price
of contractors' output is based on the assumption that they all provide an
identical service at the lowest price – a method of pricing that leaves only
a small profit margin for the builder.

Because of the great number of different materials and products that are
included in the construction of a building, any one product is only a very small
percentage of the total cost of a building. Even halving the price of a particular
component or saving a significant amount on installing it in the building will
usually make only an insignificant difference to the overall cost of construction on its own. However, as many improvements are taking place in each of
the many specialisms all the time, in aggregate change and modernization are
continually taking place in construction production, almost unnoticed and
often unremarked.

The resource-based view and VRIN

While Penrose's theory of the growth of the firm has tended to focus on the development of corporate strategy, Jay Barney (1991) discusses the characteristics of a firm's resources, which is referred to as the resource-based view (RBV). These resource-based characteristics are value (V), rarity (R), inimitability (I) and non-substitutability (N). Resources must have value, be unique or have rare features, be impossible to copy and, finally, be impossible to substitute. These resource-based characteristics have been given the acronym VRIN in management literature.

The link between growth and the VRIN characteristics of a firm's resources illustrates the contrasting nature of the construction industry compared to other sectors of the economy. In most industries, the product or service is paid for only after delivery. Until the point of sale all risk is borne by the provider. In construction, interim payments are made at various stages over many months, or even years, before production is complete, and this is seen by developers as carrying a large element of risk in order to finance the construction phase.

VRIN characteristics tend to strengthen the bargaining power of the supplier at the expense of their clients. Because developers do not encourage contractors to have VRIN characteristics, contractors appear to be backward. For example, the calls by contractors to be involved at the early stages of planning and design are often ignored by clients, who tend to prefer to wait until designs have been completed before contractors are brought into the process. In traditional contracting the design is often well advanced before builders are called upon to tender for the work. This constrains the ability of contractors to introduce innovative solutions and take advantage of their VRIN resources. Indeed, contractors and construction organizations often argue in favour of early involvement in the pre-construction phases of projects in order to introduce technical changes and improved methods of working.

It is possible that early contractor involvement in projects will become more common as the use of building information modelling (BIM) and information technology becomes more prevalent in coming years. There may be several reasons for reluctance on the part of construction clients to encourage contractors to be innovative, because it may mean ceding some control of projects to contractors before the product has even been produced. This shift towards greater control by contractors may also appear as a threat to developers by increasing the cost and risk of a project when there is little trust between the client and the contractor. This emerges as a particular problem in construction, as it is only after contracts have been signed that production takes place, in contrast to other industries, in which the supplier produces the finished product prior to sale.

Subcontractors

Much literature on the construction industry is written from the point of view of main contractors. They are seen as central to the construction production process. Main contractors organize and coordinate the materials and building component suppliers, the hiring of plant, the appointment of specialist contractors and the employing of site labour. They liaise with the architects, structural engineers, and planners and surveyors, and, of course, much of their time is taken up managing the relationship with the clients of the industry, often referred to as employers.

Subcontractors have to collaborate with other subcontractors on site as well as carrying out the instructions of the main contractor. Each specialist is only on site when required. Once there they have to carry out their contractual obligations while working alongside other subcontractors, with whom they may never have worked previously. Moreover, the actual staff carrying out the work may have been appointed only for the project, and casual and very temporary employment may be the predominant form of engagement of labour. Often the specialist contractors do not have sight of the whole contract, only that part relevant to their own contribution. Not knowing the full terms of the construction contract leaves them uncertain about the consequences of their actions and where they fit into the overall scheme and timing of the project, with the result that misunderstandings and conflicting pressures can easily arise. Indeed, specialist subcontractors tend to work simultaneously on several projects, all at different stages of completion, with different main contractors simultaneously. Subcontractors have to manage their resources working in different locations in different building teams in a wide variety of situations.

Cash flow and the problem of retention

According to Hughes, Hillebrandt and Murdoch (2000), 3 to 5 per cent of a contract may be retained by clients and developers. It can be argued that this retention protects the client to a slight extent in the event of a contractor's insolvency. It also provides the motivation for contractors to complete the work and make good any defects or snags. However, it also enables the client or employer to withhold the complete final payment in order to benefit at the expense of the main contractor, whose profit, which is a residual after all other costs have been met, is often withheld until retention payments have been made. This leaves contractors with no alternative but to delay payment to their suppliers, even though such practice is, strictly speaking, illegal, according to the Building Regulations Act (UK) of 2010. In other words, contractors and subcontractors depend on the payment of retention for their profit.

Late payment has been a perennial issue for subcontractors for many years, and, although legislation has been used in an attempt to remedy the situation, it is frequently a cause of conflict, litigation and even bankruptcy for specialist firms. Late payment adversely affects firms' cash flows and their liquidity, leading to their inability to pay their own suppliers and workforce, with the potential to bring about the collapse of their business, with problems spilling over onto completely separate projects where the specialist firms happened to be engaged – a kind of domino effect. In spite of legal penalties for late payment, specialist firms are in a weak position to enforce their claims, especially if they are dependent on the main contractor for more work in the future.

Cash flow is vital in the construction industry, particularly for the SMEs that make up the majority of the industry. Yet retention payments are designed to impact on the cash flow of contractors in several ways. When these payments are withheld or delayed the impact on contractors becomes all the greater. Withholding retention payments has several financial and economic implications for all contractors, main, sub- or specialist. Not only are they forced to lose interest on their reduced deposits in the bank, they may need to borrow to make up for late payments. Although the base rate of the Bank of England is currently very low, the interest rates contractors must pay are still significant. Withholding payments to contractors also increases the amount of working capital they require in order to pay suppliers before they themselves are paid by their employers.

Moreover, withholding or delaying payments to contractors or subcontractors limits their ability to embark on new projects until they have built up sufficient working capital funds in their own reserves. It also limits their ability to raise finance from banks, as they are seen as companies at high risk of defaulting on loans. At the same time, contractors' balance sheets are weakened by unpaid debtors, a proportion of which may become bad debts. The combination of these factors damages the reputation of contractors and represents an increased risk as far as bank lending is concerned. Because of the perceived increase in risk, contractors incur raised borrowing costs, if they are able to secure a loan at all. In addition, if they do not receive payments on time contractors are forced to pay interest on bank loans that would otherwise have been reduced.

Retention payments also imply that firms have to retain higher working capital reserves than they otherwise would require. Working capital is an additional cost that firms must set aside in order to meet their cash flow obligations. In the previous chapter we have seen that the longer the period before payments by clients, the greater the working capital requirement. As the costs facing contractors are increased through the use and abuse of retention payments, the increased cost of construction is ultimately passed on to the clients themselves, who then receive a lower level of service at higher cost than they otherwise might have expected.

In defence of retention payments

Of course, there can be legitimate reasons for postponing payments during the construction phase other than retention, but even when these delays occur they present opportunities for some firms to exploit the situation at the expense of other firms in the supply chain. In their study of the causes of payment delays, Ramachandra, Rotimi and Hyde (2015) conclude that the main causes of payment delay include contractual disputes, the consequences of a weak financial position of some firms, disputes on site, bureaucratic payment procedures and the domino effect, in which problems cascade down the supply chain. One of their key findings is that payment delays in the later stages of a project are often related to the financial weakness of the client or main contractor even before the project may have started. While these failings may account for many payment delays, whenever a payment delay occurs some firms stand to benefit while others lose, without any firm necessarily deliberately taking advantage of the situation.

The hidden costs of retention payments

Difficulties concerning late payments or withheld payments impact on cash flow, which, according to Wu, Kumaraswamy and Soo (2008), can ultimately lead to a firm's insolvency, meaning that its liabilities are greater than its assets and it has insufficient funds to meet its debt obligations. Payment delays may also slow down work on a project, further adding to costs and therefore causing productivity to be reduced, if, for example, materials cannot be delivered on time. The link between late payment and levels of productivity occurring in different countries has been described by Kadir *et al.* (2005) and Durdyev and Mbachu (2011).

Ramachandra, Rotimi and Hyde (2015) find that the most important causes of payment problems include cash flow difficulties spilling over from other projects that firms are working on simultaneously. Other causes of delayed payments include disagreements over claims, lack of capital, opportunism and the payment culture of the industry, cost overruns and lack of knowledge and experience in the field. It is difficult to see how many of these causes can be dealt with in a construction market composed of one-off projects built for individual, often non-repeating clients, leaving little room for negotiation. It is a situation in which building contractors are at a great negotiating disadvantage, especially towards the end of a project, having paid for materials and wages.

Dainty, Millett and Briscoe (2001) attribute the scepticism on the part of specialist contractors towards the uptake of innovative integrated systems of supply chain management to slow payments by main contractors. The treatment of subcontractors by main contractors forms a barrier to improved performance. Dainty, Millett and Briscoe also point out that, while there are several examples of partnering agreements between contractors and their clients, there are few between contractors and their supply chains.

Partnering agreements were introduced as a close working relationship procurement system or contractual agreement with built-in methods of resolving disputes amicably and less formally, through negotiation and adjudication rather than arbitration and the courts. Although this integration of construction management is seen as being essential if small and medium-sized firms are to contribute to improvements in performance and productivity in construction, little progress towards greater integration had been made by the end of the twentieth century, as a result of a number of barriers between contractors and their suppliers. One example of such a barrier to integration as seen by subcontractors remains the concept of retention. To overcome this barrier, Dainty, Millett and Briscoe conclude that trust between the parties is needed as much as ever. Although there has been much technical progress, and even many applications of BIM, the success of new integrated management still depends on the soft management issues of trust and integrity within the construction team, including the developer clients.

The same authors (Dainty, Millett & Briscoe 2001) also find that the lowest price remains the main criterion for the selection of subcontractors through competitive tendering, rather than the value they might add to the project. This focus on cost leads in turn to a combative relationship rather than a cooperative one. On fixed price contracts, for example, there is a fixed pot of money to be shared out between the participating firms, according to their inputs. Assessing the value of inputs is often difficult to agree between the various parties in the construction team. In terms of game theory, conflict is inherent, because construction projects involve a zero-sum game. Projects are set up in such a way that they set one player against the other. The more one firm receives, the less the others can earn from the pot, and agreement or compromise is difficult. The total gains of all the winners minus the aggregate losses of all the losers always equals zero.

To gain from a situation arising on site, not only are main contractors in a position to delay payments to subcontractors, often leading to cash flow difficulties for the subcontractors, but they may also abuse the use of retention payments at the end of projects. As Bresnan and Marshall (1999) point out, in the fragmented building process a lack of trust between clients and contractors is widespread, as well as between contractors and their subcontractors.

Chang and Ive (2007) view retention payments as a deliberate method of managing the main contractor's cash flow by clients. When "pay when paid" clauses were still permitted in law, delays in paying retention to main contractors were often used by main contractors to pass on the delay to subcontractors until the retention payment was eventually received from the client according to the practice of pay when paid. This not only reduced the effectiveness of retention payments held by clients attempting to control the behaviour of main contractors but was also at the expense of subcontractors. Although the law has changed, the weak position of subcontractors, who risk being taken off the main contractor's preferred list of suppliers, makes insisting on payment very difficult to achieve in practice.

Nevertheless, Oke and Ogunmola (2014) advocate the use of retention as a method of making professionals in the construction industry aware of the importance of delivering projects on time and to budget and as a form of protection against poor workmanship. They find that a significant relationship exists between the use of retention bonds and delivery on time and to budget, according to architects, surveyors and contractors. However, they do not mention the abuse of retention to evade full and timely payment to the contractor and they do not discuss the general poor treatment of subcontractors. Indeed, it is not clear whether or not subcontractors' views were even sought. Nevertheless, subcontractors need to overcome the difficulties faced when payments are delayed, which implies they need additional working capital to buy time to fill the void in their cash flow.

Concluding remarks

This chapter has established the relationships of developers, main contractors and subcontractors. These power relations change over the course of a project. The relative economic negotiating power of organizations in construction shift over the lifetime of a project. At the initial stages the client or employer has control over what is agreed. It is the client who decides the requirements and priorities of a project. However, once a contract has been signed, power shifts to the main contractor, who knows that replacing the main contractor becomes prohibitively expensive for the client. Negotiating power comes from the ability to impose costs on the other party, and this poses a real threat as far as the client is concerned. As clients are committed, because it is they who have purchased the site, they have more to lose than the contractor as soon as the contract has been signed.

5

PRODUCTIVITY AND
THE CONSTRUCTION MARKET

Productivity generally refers to labour productivity, although it can be used to compare the effectiveness of plant and equipment and even the performance of buildings. Labour productivity is the quantity or financial value of what is produced per person in a given period of time. As a consequence, the higher the level of productivity, the more that can be produced by a given number of people. In an economy such as the UK's, productivity tends to increase over time (see Figure 5.1) because of improvements in working practices, machinery and technology, which mean that the economy can produce the same amount with fewer people or a greater quantity of products and services with the same number of people.

Although productivity tends to increase over time, it has remained broadly flat since the global financial crisis in 2008. If productivity had continued to rise at its long-term trend rate seen before the onset of the financial crisis, according to Figure 5.1, UK productivity in 2016 would have been 20 per cent higher than it actually was.

Figure 5.2 shows that there is a considerable difference between productivity growth within sectors in the UK. Productivity has continued to gradually increase in services, which dominate. Productivity in manufacturing grew until the financial crisis of 2008 and has been stagnating since 2011. Productivity in UK construction has been broadly flat over the last 20 years, with marginal growth during the early part of the new millennium offset by the impacts of the financial crisis.

Total productivity in construction is determined by the whole team of people involved in the construction process working together. This includes

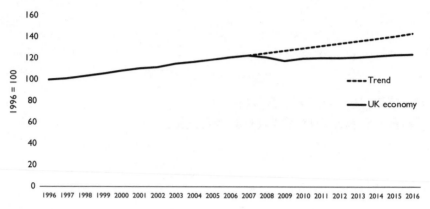

Figure 5.1 UK productivity (2006–16)
Source: ONS

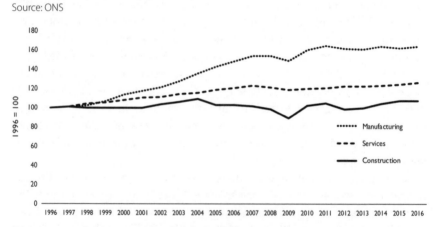

Figure 5.2 UK productivity by sector (1996–2016)
Source: ONS

all those within the supply chain, both on site and off site, and those in architectural design and the professions, major contractors, specialists, SME contractors, builders' merchants and distributors and those in plant hire and
product manufacturing. Labour productivity also depends on the plant and
machinery used and the extent to which the production process is capital-
intensive or labour-intensive. Capital intensity describes a process predom-
inantly based on using a large amount of plant and equipment, whereas a
labour-intensive process relies more on workers using their skills and simple

tools and equipment. Examples of capital-intensive processes include production that relies on automation and robotics, as in the automobile industry. Labour-intensive processes include the harvesting of certain crops in agriculture. In the construction industry, work on the existing stock tends to be labour-intensive, whereas new-build office developments and high-rise buildings are able to make use of mechanization to speed up building work because of the size and the repetitive nature of the buildings themselves. Capital-intensive methods of production increase labour productivity compared to labour-intensive methods. Nevertheless, it is possible to increase labour productivity through improvements in skills through training.

The concept of marginal productivity (MP), or, more specifically, the marginal productivity of labour, is the change in total output arising from one more person being employed, *ceteris paribus*. In other words, MP measures the change in total output when the number of people employed increases but all other inputs such as machinery, technology, energy and raw materials remain the same. MP measures the difference one more worker makes to total output. It is the difference one more worker makes to the team effort, because the marginal productivity of the last person to join the team depends on the number of people already employed. For example, there is a limit to the number of bricklayers who can be used when only one cement mixer is available. With just one bricklayer the mixer will be idle for some of the time, as it can easily provide enough cement for the first bricklayer or two, but, as more bricklayers are employed, eventually a bottleneck appears and queues will have to form to wait for the cement mixer to produce enough cement. The key point is that the difference the last person makes is not only based on the effort and ability of the last person employed but also depends on the size of the team.

Figure 5.3 illustrates a simplified example of the relationship between total output and the marginal product of the last worker employed each time individual workers are added to the workforce. The number of people employed is shown on the horizontal axis and the marginal product and total product are on the vertical axis.

To begin with, as the number of people employed increases, the total output also increases, until it reaches a peak at the fifth worker. After this point output actually declines as more workers are added. Hence, the MP equals zero at the fifth person, as total output does not increase. If more people were

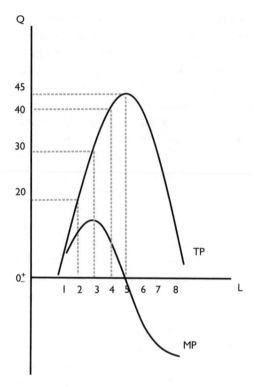

Figure 5.3 Total productivity and marginal productivity

employed, production would decline and the MP or difference each worker makes to total output would be negative.

This is because other factors become a constraint on the firm's activity. For instance, if a firm has five computers and only one person, additional employees make a considerable difference to output. However, after five employees, the computers become the limiting factor on output, not the number of people. This is what economists call the law of diminishing returns. This law states that, *ceteris paribus*, if you add more and more people to a company beyond a certain point, the increase in output is ever smaller and eventually even reduces output. Employing more people, therefore, can become counter-productive.

In Figure 5.4, when the firm employs five people its total output is 45 units, which is the maximum output possible, given its plant and machinery. At this point the marginal productivity of the last person, the fifth person, is five

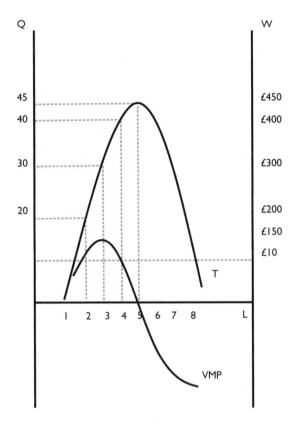

Figure 5.4 Productivity and wages

units. Assuming the aim of the firm is to employ people and make a profit, the firm has to relate the value of the marginal product of the last person employed to the wage rate. The lower the wage rate, the lower the value of the marginal product needs to be in order to cover the cost of employing that worker. The value of the marginal product (VMP) is the revenue from selling the additional output of the last worker. The VMP is calculated in two stages. First, find the marginal product (in this case five units), and, second, multiply the marginal product by the unit price at that level of output to find the VMP. For the firm to make a profit from employing the last person, the VMP must be more than or equal to the wages paid. Assuming each unit is sold for £100, then the VMP is £500.

The wages paid depend on labour demand and supply. The demand for construction labour is a derived demand. It is derived from the demand for buildings and infrastructure and repair and maintenance work. Site managers, who offer work, and the workers seeking employment are aware of the going rates for different kinds of work and skills on site. Nevertheless, the labour market is a kind of virtual auction, with workers competing with other workers, and firms competing with other firms.

This raises the question of what determines the wage paid. The actual wage paid is determined by the competition between firms in the market to attract and keep labour by offering terms and conditions that enable the firm to deliver on its contracts. Each firm has to decide how much it can afford to pay labour, and this depends on the productivity of labour, or, more accurately, the marginal productivity of labour.

Figure 5.5 shows how the demand for labour comes from the employers and is downward-sloping, reflecting the law of supply and demand that, *ceteris paribus*, the lower the wages, the more people firms would be willing to employ. In the figure the supply of labour is upward-sloping, and is comprised

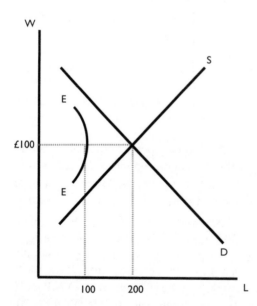

Figure 5.5 Supply and demand in the labour market

of the number of individuals with the relevant skills and qualifications who are willing and able to offer their time and effort. The higher the wages offered, *ceteris paribus*, the more people wish to participate in the market. Where the two lines intersect is the equilibrium wage. In theory, at the equilibrium wage, the number of people willing to work in construction is equal to the number of construction job vacancies.

In practice, the actual number of people employed is not as great as the equilibrium wage may imply. In Figure 5.5, the curve E–E illustrates the number of people actually employed, and this lies to the left of the supply and demand curves. Whether there is greater demand than supply or vice versa, some people will not be matched to the work available. They may have different skill sets from those required. The market for labour is fragmented, and a shortage of bricklayers does not necessarily make any difference to those skilled in trades such as plastering and drywall contracting. In any case, even though there may be a shortage of bricklayers in one area, the shortage may not be known in another area or the workers may not wish to relocate to another part of the country even for a short period. The cost of transport and time spent travelling may deter some workers from moving to where the work is on offer.

Site management skills can have a major effect on productivity by reducing the waste of time and materials. A considerable proportion of the working day is often wasted waiting for deliveries or other specialist contractors to complete their work before other specialist contractors can start on their particular work. The proportion of the working day spent waiting and unproductive is called the porosity of the working day. The aim of management is to reduce the porosity of each day to an acceptable, unavoidable and manageable proportion. For example, as a result of a lack of planning workers may be forced to wait for materials, or because the work on site cannot proceed until other work by another subcontractor has been completed. On other occasions the porosity of the working day may be unavoidable if, for example, work on site is held up because of adverse weather conditions.

As a result, productivity in construction tends to be lower than in other industries. This apparently poor performance of UK construction can be explained in terms of the nature of the industry, one-off production and an outdoor industry at the mercy of weather conditions. There are also disincentives to investment in construction to improve productivity. Labour productivity does not take account of improvements in quality, health and safety or changes to building regulations over time. Poor productivity may be a consequence of delays on site resulting from late deliveries, poor weather conditions and accidents, and delays caused by the large number of subcontractors on site, which can cause other firms to wait for work to be completed before they can get started.

Increasing the use of machinery and technology and utilizing the latest management practices are the most practical methods of improving productivity in a standard factory environment, when producing an identical product repetitively with the same group of employees. However, all these methods of improving productivity require high up-front investment, and the small size of the vast majority of firms in construction means they are not in a position to accept these challenges. Construction firms do not tend to have capital assets to be set aside as collateral. Any capital they have is usually required as working capital. The low profit margins of contractors in the construction industry and their relatively high borrowing costs imply that investment in plant and machinery and training takes a relatively long time to repay loans, and accounts for the relatively high risks associated with lending to firms in the construction industry and the relatively low level of investment in research and development and innovation in construction. For this reason, productivity in construction tends to be lower than in other industries.

Nevertheless, new ideas and innovations are constantly being introduced. Each one may be significant in its own field but, because of the complexity of the building process, they have only a limited impact on the building process. For example, several new approaches have been announced in 2018, ranging from the introduction of self-propelled management robots by a firm in California, which can tour a construction site collecting data on progress and materials used to compare with planned timing and budgets, to the use of computer vision software and artificial intelligence and working with drones on site (Quirke 2018a). Another firm in Munich, Germany, announced it had developed a robotic tool to save time and labour in erecting scaffolding (Quirke 2018b). Meanwhile, a contractor in Greece has announced the development of a new solar-powered site hut (Quirke 2018c), and a new digger using digitized hydraulics is expected to cut CO_2 emissions by half (Global Construction Review 2018). With a continuous flow of new construction products and methods coming to market, each one may increase productivity in the sector only marginally, but, taken as a whole, productivity in construction, it can be argued, is continually being improved.

Abdel-Wahab and Vogl (2011) adopt the following determinants of productivity growth, which measures the annual change in value added. These determinants are: capital (K), labour (L), energy (E) and business services (S). In addition, it is important to include total factor productivity (TFP) as a determinant of productivity improvement. TFP takes into account the increase in output over and above the increase resulting from investment in capital and labour and the other determinants, because there remains an unexplained increase in output that cannot be accounted for by capital, labour, energy and services. In other words, TFP takes into account improvements in productivity due, for example, to technical progress and improved management techniques, when firms innovate and adopt good practice they learn from other firms on site.

The annual increase in productivity in the construction industry, according to Abdel-Wahab and Vogl (2011), is lower than in other industries, although improved skills appear to have contributed to higher productivity in construction in France and the UK, as did investment in plant and machinery. However, Abdel-Wahab and Vogl found that investment in information technology had only a limited impact on productivity improvement in the period up to 2005. Since the early years of the twenty-first century the situation regarding the use of IT on site and in construction management in general has increased considerably, and the application of integrated project management techniques, including BIM, may well prove to have enhanced productivity by avoiding errors in design and clashes between services through improved design and collaborative working practices.

Two alternative management approaches to indirectly improving productivity on site are worth adding here briefly, namely lean construction and integrated project management (IPM). Both approaches can be used to contribute towards TFP in construction. Productivity is the difference between inputs and outputs, and when this difference can be increased there is an implicit increase in productivity. The movement towards lean construction is adapted from the automobile industry. Lean construction is based on lean manufacturing and attempts to reduce waste and cut unnecessary procedures, resulting in increased productivity from a widening of the difference between all the inputs and the quantity or value of output. Lean construction achieves this by seeking to eliminate certain processes or activities in managing materials, without affecting the quality, quantity and performance of output. Lean construction also advocates methods designed to reduce human error and its accompanying additional costs. In short, lean production techniques attempt to improve value for money while reducing waste.

Meanwhile, IPM brings together the management of different specialist contractors working on the same project. All the firms working on a project clearly have a common aim, namely that the project should be run in such a way that all participating firms and the client can work together to deliver a finished building or structure that allows all firms and the developer to profit from the project. Unfortunately, because of the very low profit margins, it is often almost inevitable that the main and specialist contractors will attempt to take advantage of situations that arise as the project progresses at the expense of the other firms in the team. As Baiden, Price and Dainty (2006) argue, because project teams are fragmented and temporary in nature, lasting only for the duration of the project, the coalition of firms that comprise the construction teams tend to experience adversarial relationships and a high level of mistrust, leading to individual firms pursuing strategies designed for their own self-preservation, often out of necessity.

Nevertheless, many in the building industry argue in favour of integration of the construction team, so that, by working together, the construction team can collaborate more productively and efficiently. This is not easy to achieve, especially as the actual team of people working on a building project continually changes, as different phases of the building require different skills and expertise, and staff are moved to different projects that their individual firms are working on, or, indeed, staff and labour are continually leaving to take up opportunities in other firms, only to be replaced by new employees.

Construction projects are invariably built by a coalition of specialist firms, each contributing their particular skills as and when the building process requires them. A closer relationship between the different parties from architects, through main contractors to subcontractors and the rest of the supply chain, together with the advent of building information modelling, has encouraged interest in the form of integrated project teams. Baiden, Price and Dainty (2006) define integrated project teams as having a clear set of objectives with no boundaries between the firms. They describe a number of features of integrated construction project teams, including the sharing of information, benefits and achievements in a spirit of collaboration and mutual respect. However, the construction teams surveyed tended to remain fragmented, with staff and labour working separately within their own firms. Baiden, Price and Dainty found that firms did not form a united team even when they were located in the same offices. However, by working closely together in teams, they were better able to resolve problems that arose and develop working relationships that replaced argument and distrust. Finally, Baiden, Price and Dainty found that it was possible to generate a common project culture, in which all participating firms could share similar objectives. Unfortunately, Baiden, Price and Dainty (2006) also point out that a positive culture in construction projects that might contribute towards improving productivity is unlikely to emerge, because the construction phase of most building projects is relatively short-lived and the temporary construction teams do not survive long enough to create a lasting collaborative culture.

The temporary and fragmented nature of construction teams consists of a main contractor, construction manager or management contractor, who is in charge of coordinating several specialist contractors on site. In his research on the Australian construction industry from the point of view of subcontractors, Loosemore (2014) finds that the main factors inhibiting subcontractor productivity improvement are connected with the quality of their relationships with principal contractors. Subcontractors also had little opportunity to contribute to the design at an early enough stage to facilitate ease of construction and improve productivity. This situation is made worse if the tendering process is not transparent and subcontractors are not aware of the full terms and conditions of contracts. This makes it difficult to establish trust and respect between the members of the construction team and removes incentives and opportunities for subcontractors to be innovative and improve productivity.

While there is clearly much to be learned from this research into the obstacles to innovation and improving productivity in construction, in reality the responses of firms reflect the nature of the construction process. First of all, developers set up a tender process only when they are ready to build, long after they have acquired the site and planning permission. This immediately puts the tendering process and the construction team under time pressure to start on site and complete the building process as quickly as they can. However, it is virtually impossible to plan a project efficiently under these circumstances. As a result, there exists a culture of blame in construction, as can be seen from the many examples of poor working practice, described by Loosemore (2014). This is not to say that Loosemore is mistaken but, rather, that the underlying cause of relatively low productivity may lie elsewhere, long before the construction team is formed.

One remedy frequently proposed for construction productivity being lower than manufacturing productivity is off-site manufacturing. Although it is appealing to think that shifting production from on site to prefabrication under factory conditions would help to raise productivity, there are still several problems to be overcome. We take housing as an example to explain some of the difficulties involved.

CASE STUDY 2: OFF-SITE MANUFACTURING FOR HOUSING

The conventional business model in UK construction uses labour, capital, plant, tools and materials and off-site manufactured products to produce bespoke buildings and structures. However, historically, there have been criticisms regarding the time, cost and quality of what is built in the construction industry. In addition, there have also been concerns regarding productivity in construction and slow productivity growth over time within the construction industry. Figure 5.6 shows that, between 1996 and 2016, productivity within the UK economy measured by output per job rose by 24 per cent, at a rate of 1.2 per cent per year. However, over the same period construction productivity rose only by 7.7 per cent, a rate of 0.4 per cent per year.

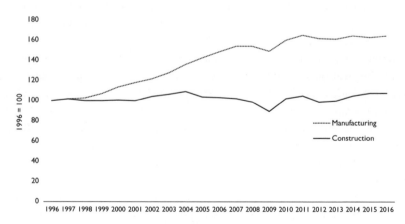

Figure 5.6 Productivity in UK manufacturing and construction (1996–2016)
Source: ONS

One potential solution that has been suggested to overcome the problem of low productivity in the construction industry is to build the majority of the building or structure away from the construction site, off site, in a manufacturing facility. Off-site construction has existed for over 80 years in various forms, and it uses standardized, factory-produced, pre-assembled modules or systems of components that may provide many benefits compared to on-site manufacture. It is argued that the benefits of off-site manufacturing include fewer defects, faster construction, time savings, improved energy efficiency, less waste, greater scope for recycling and reduction in the transportation cost of materials. In addition, a consistent lack of traditional trade skills in construction has also been raised as a concern within standard construction. Many people also argue that off-site manufacturing reduces the labour content of construction, especially the cost of labour on site. Furthermore, off-site manufacturing is also seen as a possible method of improving poor productivity levels and productivity growth within construction compared to industrial productivity, which increased by 64.6 per cent, at a rate of 3.2 per cent per year, between 1996 and 2016 in the rest of manufacturing, according to the ONS data shown in Figure 5.7. However, if a substantial proportion of construction activity were taken off site, into a manufacturing facility, then the value of that activity would be in manufacturing rather than construction. Although on-site activity would then require fewer people, it would also be adding less value on site. As a result, it is possible that construction productivity could actually fall with the increased use of off-site manufacturing.

Off-site construction in 2016 accounted for only 10 per cent of house building in the UK. However, the UK government stated openly in 2017 that it saw off-site manufacturing as the future for construction, and, in its White Paper *Industrial Strategy: Building a Britain Fit for the Future*, published in November (HM Government 2017), the government states that five UK government departments will adopt a presumption in favour of off-site construction by 2019.

One of the key opportunities for off-site manufacturing is in the housing sector, as the government has ambitious targets to raise the level of house building activity in England only from 237,000 net additional homes per year in 2016/17 to 300,000 homes per year by 2022. In addition, the Construction Industry Training Board (CITB) reported in April 2017 that off-site manufacturing may also provide opportunities for construction in the infrastructure, commercial and industrial sectors by taking advantage of the standardization of parts of the structure across multiple buildings from the design stage.

However, a key hindrance to new investment in off-site manufacturing in house building is the volatility of demand in the sector. Within construction more generally, volatile demand also acts as a disincentive to invest, and this is exacerbated by the low profit margins in the industry, which constrain the finance available for investment.

Within house building, private housing starts fell by 71.1 per cent in just two years as a result of the financial crisis (see Figure 5.7). The standard UK house builder business model, which involves subcontracting out the majority of labour, materials, plant and tools, enables firms to reduce costs in line with demand. However, a reliance on off-site construction would mean high investment up front for a long-term rate of return that may not be realized, and the investing firm would then be left with the risk of high fixed costs that it may not be able to cover.

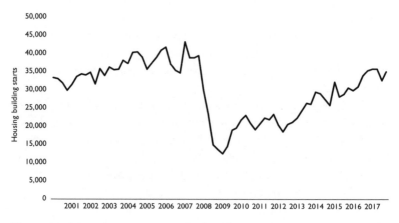

Figure 5.7 Private housing starts in England (2001–17)
Source: DCLG

Manufacturing does not deal well with sharp falls in demand, on account of the fixed costs of borrowing to invest (namely interest payments and repayment schedules) in machinery and materials. It would be difficult to justify investment in manufacturing en masse when sharp falls in demand are expected with each downturn.

Off-site manufacturing could potentially make a significant impact in areas of house building that are less volatile and when the developer is also the owner. When this is the case the owner may take a long-term interest in the houses being built, so that the short-term fall in demand during downturns is less of an issue. Examples of this include house building for the private rental sector and housing associations, which build affordable and social housing.

In addition, there are also cultural aspects that impact on the way in which new homes are built in the UK. According to the ONS, 56 per cent of the house building market in 2017 was new-build housing while the remaining 44 per cent was the repair, maintenance and improvement (RM&I) work on the existing stock. New house building accounted for less than 1 per cent of the housing stock on average in England during 2016/17. As a result, England has a small new-build housing market and a large market for work on existing stock. As off-site manufacturing is – by definition – manufacturing, it lends itself more towards the construction of standardized products, which means that it is much more suited to new build and much less for bespoke, labour-intensive RM&I activity.

Japan already uses off-site manufacturing to a greater extent in house building than in England, but it has a very different housing market. In Japan 980,000 homes were built in 2013, compared with 124,960 in England. In addition, 121,397 homes were demolished in Japan in 2013, compared with only 12,060 in England. In Japan 3 per cent of the housing stock was built before 1945. However, in England the equivalent figure is 37 per cent of the housing stock. As a result, the housing market in Japan has a culture of renewing the housing stock and there is high demand for new homes, while in England the interest has primarily been in existing homes, with a focus on the repair, maintenance and improvement of them.

Furthermore, the Japanese house-building market is much bigger and less volatile than the house-building market in England. Private house building starts in Japan fell 37 per cent thanks to the global financial crisis, and even after the recession private house building was still 800,000 homes per year. This contrasts sharply with the 71 per cent fall in private housing starts in England at the nadir of the house-building market as a result of the financial crisis.

If off-site manufacturing were to become mainstream in house building for sale in the UK, it would be more likely if demand in the UK housing market was more stable and if there was a substantial shift in the housing culture and market towards new-build homes.

Concluding remarks

The lack of productivity growth within UK construction can be explained in two key ways: the first is related to the nature of the industry; and the second is related to hindrances to investment. Given that the definition of labour productivity is the value or volume of activity per worker or hour worked, it does not take account of improvements in quality, health and safety or changes to building regulations over time. However, if the volume of construction activity per worker is the same but the quality has improved or the construction industry is suffering fewer injuries and fatalities, then that is surely a good thing. Furthermore, given that labour productivity is activity per worker or per hour worked, the easiest way to increase productivity is to use machinery and technology and utilize the latest management practices, which is most practical to do within a standard factory environment when producing a generic product with the same group of employees. The key issue with the construction industry, as highlighted in Chapter 2, is that the construction industry produces a bespoke product each time with different groups of employees across different supply chains. Chapter 1 has highlighted the extent of fragmentation in the construction supply chain and Chapter 3 highlights the low profit margins in the construction industry, the volatility in activity in the sector and the method of dealing with risk in a volatile sector (focusing on short-term flexibility and pushing the risk down the fragmented supply chain to smaller firms). However, all the key methods of improving productivity highlighted above, such as improvements in skills, management, machinery or technology, all require high up-front investment, and SME firms are the least able to deal with these given that they have low profit margins and less, and more costly, access to borrowing from financial institutions, reflecting the risk regarding the return on the lending for investment.

If the government wishes to see considerable improvements in productivity within construction, then it has a key part to play. Government accounts for one-quarter of all spending on construction within the UK, according to the Office for National Statistics. As a consequence, if, as the largest purchaser and consumer of construction, government's focus on procuring construction is primarily on cost, then construction for the largest client will occur at low profit margins, thus hindering the funds necessary to invest. However, if government were to purchase construction with a focus on value and quality, then this would enable profit margins that enable investment in new machinery, technology and advanced management practices. In addition, as the largest client, if government cuts its construction spending at the same time that the private sector stops construction spending, for instance during a recession, then this exacerbates volatility in the sector and incentivizes firms within construction to focus only on the short term, subcontracting out for flexible labour and avoiding risk rather than investing. However, if government were to invest in construction over the long term, with a focus on the long-term needs of the economy and ignoring economic cycles, it would reduce volatility in the sector and allow construction firms to plan for the long term, allowing for up-front investment in machinery, technology and advanced management practices.

6

THE GAME OF CONSTRUCTION

The fragmented nature of the UK construction industry has been highlighted in Chapter 1. The construction industry consists of different types of skills, in firms ranging from architects, consultants, contractors, plant and tool hire. For the construction client, all these firms need to combine in an efficient manner within a project to produce a building that meets the client's requirements. On site, even within each contractor, a large number of different construction trades and skills from different specialists or subcontractors need to be organized to come together for each distinct piece of work within the project. It would not be practical for the client, who is merely interested in the end product, to organize, monitor and manage all these organizations. It is essential, therefore, to procure the construction process in an efficient manner so as to overcome the problems of fragmentation and the number of different skills needed. This is achieved by putting the work out to tender to main contractors. As a result, to win the right to undertake a project, main contractors are involved in an auction.

Auctions may take various forms. The majority of auctions sell directly to consumers, whether they be for art, second-hand cars or any goods on eBay. When auctioning property, the auctioneer tends to start with a low base price to incentivize a person to make a first bid. Other bidders then enter the auction by bidding a higher amount and increasing the price based upon their willingness to pay. Eventually the highest bid wins, when no one else is prepared to offer an even higher bid. This form of auction is called an open-ascending bid auction, or, more commonly, an English auction, in which the bidding is based on increasing bids. However, the most common form of auction in the construction industry is called a first-price sealed-bid auction. In this type of auction, contractors submit their bids to the client in sealed envelopes by a certain deadline. The sealed bids are then opened, and, in general, the lowest bid by a reputable contractor is generally selected, assuming that all bids represent approximately equivalent solutions that meet the client's proposal. In practice, individual bids may vary from contractor to contractor in terms of the specification of materials and products, quality, energy efficiency, need for long-term maintenance and other factors that differentiate each bid by different contractors. For example, during the procurement of the facilities for the 2012 London Olympics, a number of non-price criteria were indicated by the Olympic Delivery Authority, which then used a number of criteria other than price to select main contractors based on the need for the work to be done by a deadline that could not be extended and the client's focus on quality and long-term legacy. However, even in this case, price was clearly still a major factor.

Before submitting their bid the main contractors approach their own contacts and suppliers to find out the prices of employing their specialist suppliers or subcontractors. On winning the tender, the winning contractor then subcontracts different elements of the work to its subcontractors and various suppliers.

Each contractor's bid price is based on the estimated total of all the prices of its specialist subcontractors, plus the cost of materials, plant and tool hire to be used in the construction. The price submitted by the contractors includes a mark-up by the main contractor that covers the main contractor's costs and profits and also includes for a contingency sum to allow for the unexpected, as construction costs are uncertain.

However, as mentioned earlier, the business model of main contractors is based upon winning projects and managing them while the majority of activity is subcontracted. Therefore, the main contractor's incentive is to win as many projects as possible, to increase revenue by making a profit on each project, rather than selecting only a few projects that may promise a higher mark-up or profit margin on a smaller value of sales.

The consequence of main contractors utilizing a business model focusing on winning and managing as many projects as possible is that they often quote a cost for a project that leaves them a low profit margin in order to increase the probability of winning the bid. However, the result of this strategy is that main

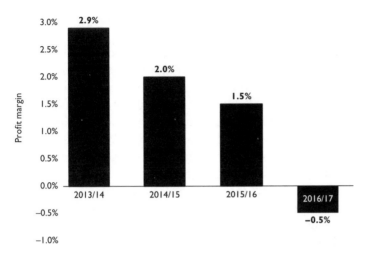

Figure 6.1 Average profit margin of the top ten UK contractors (2013/14–2016/17)
Source: London Stock Exchange

contractors consistently have low margins on projects, and often, despite high construction demand, end up with negative margins when a small increase in the cost of inputs has meant that their margins are so small they end up losing money on the project, with a negative profit margin. This can be seen, for example, in Figure 6.1. Despite four consecutive years of rising demand in construction, as measured by construction output, the average pre-tax profit margin of the ten largest UK construction firms declined steadily between 2013/14 and 2016/17, and was even negative in 2016/17.

Main contractors also suffer from what Capen, Clapp and Campbell (1971) refer to as the "winner's curse". The winner's curse was highlighted by engineers working in the oil industry, who found that auctions for oil leases for the right to extract oil in the United States' outer continental shelf led to winning bidders consistently overestimating returns. They may have won the auction but they went on to lose money on the price they paid for the oil lease. In principle, the value of the lease is the same to all bidders, but some bidders may be tempted to overestimate the value of the lease and bid a higher price than the others in the market. Unfortunately, the winner than discovers that it has overpaid for the lease when it finds that it cannot make a profit from the amount paid in the auction – hence the winner's curse.

Likewise, in construction, each main contractor bidding for a construction contract has its own estimate of the construction cost at the point in time when it bids and what mark-up it would like to add. Some of the bidding contractors may bid too high due to an overestimation of the costs and/or the mark-up they would like to earn, in which case they do not win the contract. However, some firms may bid too low, as they underestimate the costs involved and/or apply no, or a low, mark-up. Their bid for the work is so low that they win the contract, only to discover that they make a loss on the project. Furthermore, going forward, on future tenders the competing contractors that did not win the original contract are increasingly likely to lower their bids for work to ensure that they also win some contracts. In economic theory, the winner's curse cannot exist if all the bidders are rational. However, acting rationally is difficult with imperfect information on the availability and cost of inputs and the value of competing bids.

Given low and negative margins on many contracts, main construction firms need to find areas in which they can sustain themselves. If the revenue is determined by the contract signed with the client, then the only other area of opportunity is on the cost side of the firm, and this is achieved by utilizing the power asymmetry on the contract with subcontractors. Power asymmetry is the unequal power and control that large firms have over their relatively small suppliers. Major contractors are the only firms able to win many projects, owing to their size, access to funds and their ability to manage the projects, as the majority of activity is subcontracted out by the large firms to smaller firms. These smaller firms are dependent on the relatively few large contractors for work. As a result, main contractors are in a position to make their subcontractors wait for payment for work with long payment terms, so as to delay incurring the costs, while enjoying the benefits of the income from the client.

Main contractors may also hold onto retentions, amounts of money held back to ensure that work by subcontractors is carried out to the required standard. This protects the main contractor against defective work. Retentions by the main contractor usually involve the main contractor holding a proportion of the subcontractor's fee (generally 5–10%), half of which is paid following the contract and the remainder paid after a period that allows for checking the quality of work (up to 24 months). However, the use of retention is open to abuse, if main contractors withhold a part of the retention, or the entirety, for long periods, which adversely affects the smaller subcontractors.

Theoretically, these subcontractors can use legal recourse, but this is very expensive for often cash-constrained small firms, especially as there is no guarantee of winning the case. Moreover, the subcontractors may be reliant on a main contractor for more work in the future, which could be put at risk by legal action.

By underpricing their work and bidding a low price, main contractors may need to return to their suppliers and ask them to reduce their prices further. The subcontractor or supplier may be unwilling or unable to make a price reduction. The threat of a major contractor substituting a subcontractor with a new firm may lead to what is often referred to as a Dutch auction. In essence, the term "Dutch auction" refers to a situation in which firms bid lower and lower in order to ensure that they win the contract. Such auctions can also occur when main contractors play existing subcontractors off against each other in order to put pressure on both subcontractors to lower their prices and, in the process, the main contractors' costs, increasing the profits of the main contractor at the expense of its subcontractors.

The issues revolving around payment, retentions, cost reductions and delays through the supply chain often lead to disputes. A number of methods have been devised to resolve differences that can arise. These include arbitration, adjudication, mediation and, as a last resort, litigation. In arbitration, both sides in a dispute agree to abide by the binding decision of the arbitrator. In adjudication, if the adjudicator's decision is not accepted by all parties, it becomes an interim decision depending on confirmation or rejection by a court. A third method of dispute resolution is mediation, whereby the parties to a dispute attempt to negotiate an acceptable resolution with the help of the mediator. If none of the above has resolved the issues, then it is always possible for firms to take the dispute to court. Unfortunately, litigation is time-consuming and expensive, and in reality firms try to avoid taking the matter to court in order to avoid having the dispute made public, as publicity can damage a firm's reputation, making it unlikely that the firms involved will ever be able to work together again.

Bringing together firms across the whole construction supply chain involves procurement systems, contracts, changes in contracts and dispute resolution procedures. For the construction process to work collaboratively and smoothly it is assumed that the firms involved understand the implications of the terms of agreement in their contracts and receive appropriate professional legal advice. Unfortunately, as 86 per cent of employment is in small and medium-sized enterprises, the owners may simply not have the resources in terms of knowledge, experience, time or finance to prepare themselves adequately for the roles and risks they undertake. Inevitably, when variations are needed and unplanned changes arise, causing uncertainty, some firms will tend to deal with the situation better than others. As a result, although they may all play according to the same rules and contract terms, some firms are able to take advantage of the situation more than others. For this reason, an understanding of game theory can provide insights into how individuals and firms behave within construction.

Like any game, the economics of game theory involves situations in which there are only a few players. The actions of any one player will affect and be affected by the actions of the other players. The initial origins of game theory are much debated, but it was initially developed as a separate field of research by the mathematician John von Neumann in 1928, and was first applied to economics in 1944 in a book he co-authored with the economist Oskar Morgenstern called *The Theory of Games and Economic Behavior* (von Neumann & Morgenstern 1944). Game theory is not a model in the standard economic sense but a framework to simplify the world that is used to assess the rational course of action given at least two parties or "players", a given situation, potential decisions they may make and a set of potential consequences, also known as outcomes. Therefore, it allows us to anticipate the best result possible.

In its most basic form it has only two players and two possible decisions for each player and is a zero-sum game. A zero-sum game is one in which no income is created or lost and, as a result, whatever one player wins the other player loses. It is a simplification of the world because, in a zero-sum game, an optimal situation is always possible. However, the majority of games that occur in real life are not zero-sum games, given that it is possible for all players to win, or, conversely, all players may lose. In the construction industry, the majority of issues that can be analysed using game theory are also non-zero-sum games and, in general, illustrate that, at least theoretically, collaboration between all players would achieve better results for all the players involved.

The most famous example of game theory is called the prisoner's dilemma, developed by Merrill Flood and Melvin Dresher in 1951. In this game two potential criminals have been arrested by the police. The police believe that

		Potential criminal 2	
		Confess	Deny
Potential criminal 1	Confess	5, 5	0, 10
	Deny	10, 0	2, 2

Figure 6.2 The prisoner's dilemma

one or both of them are guilty of a crime. However, they do not have sufficient evidence to prove it. The two potential criminals are kept apart, in separate cells, without the ability to communicate between themselves. In this situation, there are four possible options. If neither prisoner confesses, then they will both be convicted for two years. If both confess to their crime, then both will be sentenced to five years in prison. However, if one prisoner confesses to his crime and the other does not, then the prisoner who confessed will be set free, whereas the prisoner who did not confess will be convicted for ten years. This is illustrated in Figure 6.2.

As with any game, there is a high dependence within game theory on the risk preferences of those involved in the game. Some players may be risk-averse while others may be prepared to gamble, taking on greater risk. Attitudes towards risk influence the strategies that individuals and firms adopt, a strategy being a set of linked decisions based on an underlying preference. As a result, firms may take decisions that are consistent with their strategic preferences. There are generally two broad strategies, maximax and maximin, which summarize the two main sets of tactics that may be adopted. Based on attitudes towards risk, some firms prefer taking on risk because they are willing and able to accept the consequences. Other firms are risk-averse, which means they seek to reduce the level of risk associated with the projects they undertake. The maximax strategy is optimistic and willing to take on risk. It therefore offers a higher rate of return than maximin, which is a risk-averse strategy that takes into account the risks involved and selects only those options that remain after eliminating those options with risky outcomes. Maximin strategies therefore offer a lower potential rate of return than maximax strategies.

If we assume that both potential criminals, or players, are rational, then they will chose the strategy that leads to the least amount of time in prison.

With regard to the above matrix, each prisoner is looking to minimize his or her prison time. Since potential criminal 1 does not know whether the other player has confessed or not, he or she will assume not. If potential criminal 1 does not confess, then he or she does not confess either, then both will go to prison for two years, the better of the two options. However, if potential criminal 1 confesses, he or she goes free while his or her partner goes to prison for ten years. But what happens if potential criminal 2 confesses? In this case, if potential criminal 1 does not confess, then he or she goes to prison for ten years, but, if potential criminal 1 does confess, then he or she goes to prison for five years. As a result, confession would be the better option. However, this assumes that the potential criminals know what the other is going to do. In the dilemma outlined initially, both are kept separate and do not know what the other would do. In this case, the equilibrium is for both to confess. This is the strategy that minimizes the chance of the other player winning. In effect, betraying the other player offers a greater reward than cooperating with him or her, given the uncertainty regarding what the other player will do, and, as a consequence, self-interested rational players lead both players to betray each other despite a better outcome for both had they both denied the crime.

This is called the Nash equilibrium, named after the mathematician John Nash. The Nash equilibrium describes a situation in which all people in a group make the best decision for themselves based upon what they think the others will do. Neither they nor the others can do better by changing strategy. So, in the case of the prisoner's dilemma, keeping quiet is never a good idea, whatever the other person chooses. The Nash equilibrium helps economists understand how decisions that are good for individuals can be situations that are not good for the group.

The interest in this framework is, clearly, not in helping prisoners but in helping to understand how the construction industry works and why firms within the industry make certain decisions, and it is here that we introduce what we have chosen to call the contractor's dilemma (Figure 6.3). Reflecting the lack of trust in construction, it is necessary to avoid actions that could be undermined by the decisions of others. It is, therefore, often the case that both maximin and maximax strategies amount to taking the same strategic decision.

In the contractor's dilemma, a main contractor already has two subcontractors working for it on one phase of work on a project, each earning £6 million

		Subcontractor 2	
		Accept fee cut	Refuse fee cut
Subcontractor 1	Accept fee cut	5, 5	10, 0
	Refuse fee cut	0, 10	7, 7

Figure 6.3 The contractor's dilemma

for the activity. In a subsequent phase of work, it would be easier for the main contractor to work with existing subcontractors due to the expense and difficulties of finding a new, additional subcontractor. Moreover, there may be issues of uncertainty and trust in the quality of work with a new subcontractor. Furthermore, subcontractors may also prefer to work for a main contractor in which they can trust, as a result of working for it previously, and may not have the option of picking and choosing who they work for. In this case, the main contractor may specify a new lower price at which it would anticipate the subcontractors could work at, and try to play the subcontractors off against each another. Again, assuming that the subcontractors do not communicate with each other then, as with the prisoner's dilemma, there are four possible outcomes.

If both firms accept the cut in fee, then both will continue to work for the main contractor but earning less than previously: £5 million each. If subcontractor 1 refuses the fee cut but subcontractor 2 accepts the fee cut, then subcontractor 1 will not work for the main contractor subsequently, and earns zero, but subcontractor 2 will be paid £10 million: £5 million for the work initially offered and £5 million for the activity initially expected to be undertaken by subcontractor 1. The converse is also true. If subcontractor 2 refuses the fee cut but subcontractor 1 accepts the fee cut, then subcontractor 2 will not work for the main contractor subsequently and earns zero, but subcontractor 1 will be paid £10 million, which includes the activity it takes over from subcontractor 2 during the next phase. However, if both subcontractors refuse the fee cut, then the main contractor will be forced to offer a higher price to retain either or both subcontractors to do the work, or tender for new subcontractors, which would entail additional resource in terms of time and cost. In this scenario, each subcontractor could earn £7 million for activity in the next phase.

The best strategy, given no communication between the contractors, is for both to accept the fee cuts and both to continue working with the main contractor, as neither may be in the position to refuse to work. However, this relies on two key assumptions. First, it assumes that there is no communication; and, second, it assumes that the game is played only once. With the first assumption, theoretically, if the subcontractors were able to communicate, they would be able to decide on a strategy together that would ensure that the final result is the more lucrative outcome for both the firms by earning £7 million each. However, this would be considered collusion in the sector, and is illegal. In addition, if the second assumption were to be relaxed as well, and there were many games with a similar situation, then subcontractors could, theoretically, work together and arrange for one firm to win all the work in one game and then for the other firm to win all the work in the next game, both leading to higher earnings than would have occurred in the initial contractor's dilemma case. However, this type of collusion between firms in an industry is also illegal.

The contractor's dilemma example is applicable not just to the relationship between the main contractor and the subcontractors but also to the relationship between large clients (which are experienced and knowledgeable) and main contractors that wish to consistently win work from the same client. In this case, it is the main contractors that have to accept lower fees for consistent work, which then may lead to problems of contractor's dilemma down the supply chain. However, again, in this example, if the assumptions are relaxed, then main contractors could, theoretically, collude to ensure that both could gain financially – and, although this is illegal, it has occurred in the recent past.

Game theory may also be used to analyse disputes as well. In this theoretical example, called the driver's choice, two motorists are driving quickly towards each other on a narrow road. Both want to survive but neither wants to feel as though he or she was the driver who had to move out of the way. If neither driver turns off the road, then both drivers will die. If both drivers turn, then both drivers will survive, but both will also feel they have given way to the other driver, because they were forced to concede. If one driver turns and the other does not, then both survive and one driver feels the excitement of victory over the other, not having had to turn. Meanwhile, the other driver feels disappointment that he or she turned whereas the other driver

		Driver 2	
		Turn	Drive straight
Driver 1	Turn	3, 3	2, 5
	Drive straight	5, 2	0, 0

Figure 6.4 The driver's choice

did not. This game is illustrated in Figure 6.4. In this game, if both drivers drive straight, then the outcome is 0 for both, as the cars crash. If both drivers turn, then the value for both is 3, having survived, and, although they may be disappointed at having had to turn off the road, this is only equivalent to the disappointment of the other driver, who made the same move. If driver 1 turns but driver 2 drives straight, then the value for driver 1 is 2, while driver 2 achieves 5. Conversely, if driver 2 turns but driver 1 drives straight on, then the value for driver 2 is 2 while driver 1 achieves 5.

The key difference between the driver's choice example and both the prisoner's dilemma and the contractor's dilemma is that, in the driver's choice, there are two potential optimum solutions rather than one. Either driver driving straight is an optimum strategy for one driver only, as long as the other driver turns, which results in the outcomes 5, 2 or 2, 5.

Again, we can take the driver's choice example from game theory and apply it to the construction industry, in order to look at a dispute between a major client and a main contractor (Figure 6.5). In this game, let us assume there has been a significant delay to a construction project, which is of great concern to the client as it had a specific deadline for the project to be launched. However, the contractor states that this delay has occurred because of changes in specification initiated by the client during construction, which the client denies. The client argues that the delay is because of issues from the contractor. As a consequence, there is a dispute.

In this situation, there are two ways for the contractor to act. It may continue as per normal or it could, in the short term, work overtime and devote additional resource to the project. On the other hand, the client also has a choice. It could delay the launch and give a time extension to the contractor, or it could state that the contractor must work to the original deadline. In

		Contractor	
		No overtime	Overtime
Client	Extension time	2, 4	3, 3
	No extension time	1, 1	4, 2

Figure 6.5 Clients and contractors

this case, if the contractor does not work overtime and there is not a time extension from the client, the project will be completed, but late, and miss the launch date. There are two realistic, optimum solutions. Either the client gives the contractor an extension for the project, allowing the contractor to work at the current pace and still get the project completed by the revised deadline; or, if the contractor works overtime on the project to ensure that it is completed on time without the client making any changes in timing, the project could be completed in a timely manner at the contractor's expense. In essence, one of the two players of the game will have to compromise to ensure a successful project, given the original dispute and the potential outcomes. If the client does not give the contractor an extension period and the contractor is not willing to pay overtime, then the project is at high risk of being late, or never finished at all in the worst case. Adjudication and litigation are unrealistic at this point (although possible following completion of the project), given the impending deadline.

Concluding remarks

Overall, the risk involved in construction and the fragmentation of the construction supply chain leads to a business model in which there is a power asymmetry in the construction sector. Projects and programmes often take years, and there are many unknowns that are difficult to know but must be estimated to determine the cost. The incentives for the main contractor are to win as many projects as possible, although these often result in low or negative margins, and so, to ensure that main contractors are sustainable, methods for overcoming or dealing with the low and negative margins are pushed onto the supply chain. Subcontractors and suppliers often have to deal with the consequences or end up in resource-intensive disputes. Theoretically, collaboration would lead to better solutions for all firms within construction. However, the lack of trust in the construction industry means that the incentives are to take advantage of any power asymmetry that exists, leading to a suboptimal solution for all firms.

7

THE UNDERLYING CAUSES OF CONFLICT IN CONSTRUCTION

The interests of buyers differ considerably from those of sellers. For instance, buyers want a low price while sellers want a high price, but are these disagreements over price accommodated by market forces? Conflict is present in many transactions across the economy. Conflicts may arise when buying or selling a car, agreeing wages to be paid or negotiating an exit from the European Union. The different parties have different interests, and disputes are common. In construction projects, disputes arise for a number of specific reasons. For example, according to Sithole (2016), disputes can arise over contractual issues, management problems, disagreements between people, disputes over payment or quality, issues arising out of design problems and issues of communication and misunderstanding.

No construction contract can possibly predict all the problems that may arise in the course of a project. In one sense, these disputes are all symptoms of a central conflict underlying all commercial relationships between the actors in any production process; in the case of construction projects, for example, disagreements between contractors, subcontractors, developers and suppliers. These issues certainly form the specific details of many disputes that arise on site, where contractors and clients may continue working together on the production process even when they are in dispute. This is in contrast to many other industries, such as manufacturing, where production takes place prior to the client purchasing the finished product and where disagreements can be resolved without affecting the customer directly – with the exception of internal disputes between management and the workforce, when strikes may delay delivery of the finished product.

To resolve the many disputes that arise in the construction industry, there are a number of ways of dealing with them, including arbitration, adjudication and mediation, all designed to avoid the expense of litigation in court, which is seen as a costly last resort. Before going to the expense of litigation arbitrators, adjudicators or mediators may be appointed as a means of resolving matters more speedily and at lower cost than using the formal legal system.

One of the underlying sources of conflict in the construction supply chain is the result of disagreement over the share of the overall price charged in return for the risk, effort and reward for undertaking particular tasks by the various parties involved. There is no one agreed formula for settling disagreements, especially if work has not gone according to plan. To gain an understanding of the conflict between the parties involved in the production process, we need to consider two concepts in particular, namely value added and surplus value.

Whenever production takes place, materials are used. These are the physical inputs, such as raw materials, manufactured components and other ingredients, that are needed in the process. If the total cost of all the materials comes to £50,000 and the finished goods are sold at £75,000, then the value added to the material inputs is £25,000. All the expenses of the firm, other than the cost of materials, must be covered by the value added, including wages and profits. The higher wages are, the less is available for profits. This is an example of a zero-sum game, because the total of gains less the total of losses is always equal to zero. The workers may not always agree that wages should be cut in order to leave more for profits, and, similarly, the owners of the firm may not agree that profits are sufficient if high wages prevent the owners and managers from having an incentive to invest as much as they would like in the firm's expansion. The conflict between the two sides, the owners and the workers, is always present. How the value added is divided between the two sides is an ongoing source of disagreement.

Value added has to fund more than the wages of the workers and the profits of the firm's owners. A firm's profit is the source of the funding used to pay for investment. Investment is paid for by retaining profits from profits made in the past, and these are topped up with borrowing. All other expenses also come out of the money remaining after wages have been paid, including rent, interest and other head office costs.

As we noted above, the two key concepts are value added and surplus value. Together, they reveal the conflicting relationships between players. In the tendering process used to appoint contractors and subcontractors before construction can begin, a price is agreed between the client or employer and the contractor. From the point of view of the contractor, surplus is what remains after materials and direct labour have been paid. Direct labour includes the workers who actually carry out the building work. This leaves money to pay for rent, interest payments and profits, all items that are paid out of the surplus.

If the selling price of a new build office block is equal to both the cost of all the material inputs that were used in its construction and the cost of the wages that were paid to the labour that built it, then there would be nothing left to pay all other expenses and profits. These remaining items of expenditure include rent to be paid for the contractor's head office, interest to be paid for loans to purchase plant and machinery and other assets the contractor may own and the materials to be purchased before payment is made by the client and, finally, profit to the firm to ensure it can continue to remain in business. The profit is the residual after all other expenses have been paid. A business that makes no profit will not survive.

A simple example will illustrate the point (see Figure 7.1). Assume the selling price of a building is £100 million. This amount is distributed among all the stakeholders in the building process, including the landlord of the building firm's own offices. Assume the materials cost £45 million. The materials are the inputs into the construction process. They are transformed by labour into the finished building. When the building is sold for £100 million, the *value added* to the materials by labour is £55 million, the selling price less the cost of material inputs. By virtue of working on the materials, labour has added £55 million to the value of the bought-in materials and components, now assembled and finished. However, the labour wages actually paid amounts only to £30 million. This leaves a *surplus* of £25 million, which is the amount left over after materials and wages have been paid.

If wages had been £5 million higher, then the surplus would have been reduced to £20 million: the higher the wages, the lower the surplus. It is therefore in the interests of employers to keep wages as low as they can, but it is in the interests of the workers to be paid as much as possible. As materials are priced by builders' merchants and manufacturers and other costs such as energy costs and interest rates are beyond the control of the contractors,

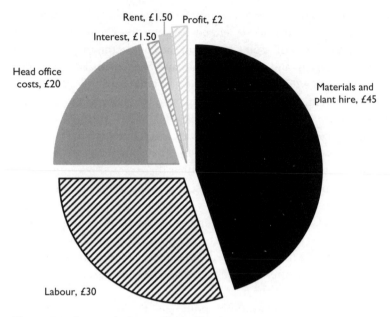

Rent, £1.50   Profit, £2

Interest, £1.50

Head office costs, £20

Materials and plant hire, £45

Labour, £30

Figure 7.1 Costs including profits (millions)

labour is in the weakest position to negotiate and defend wage rates when contractors need to cut costs, especially when there is unemployment.

The remaining difference between the selling price and the total cost of materials, products and wages is the surplus value produced by labour. It is this surplus that pays for rent, interest and all other expenses. From the firm's perspective, it also covers the profits, which are an expense like any other as far as the firm is concerned. Indeed, if, and only if, a firm makes a profit will it have to pay tax. In other words, tax also comes out of the surplus after materials and wages have been paid and before profits. Wages come out of value added while rent, interest and profits are shared out of surplus value.

Unfortunately, there is no one agreed method for sharing out the gains from a project. More often than not the share of the profits from a project depends on the negotiating skills and strengths of the various firms and the market conditions at the time. For example, if there is a shortage of electricians, then electricians will be in a position to demand a higher price or simply move their business to a new client willing to pay that higher price.

Value added and value added tax

Every production process transforms raw materials and manufactured inputs into finished goods and services. This transformation process occurs in most sectors of the economy: minerals, agriculture, energy, manufacturing, construction and even some service industries. At every stage of the production process the firms involved use inputs from other firms, which they work on. They may, for example, make components that then complete their output, which they, in turn, sell on to a firm that then takes the semi-finished goods to the next stage. Production is a very complex process, often involving components being worked on in one location before being moved to another factory, often in another country. The more complex the product is, the more it crosses national borders in the course of its manufacture.

This occurs, for example, in aircraft manufacture, automobile production and medical equipment production. Not all industries are necessarily as fragmented. For example, clothing, agricultural produce and publishing are often produced in one location. What all firms have in common is that they transform inputs into goods and services that they sell at a higher price than the cost of the material inputs.

In construction, the material inputs are assembled on site to become buildings and structures. A building, for example, is comprised of a large number of elements, from doors and windows, heaters and boilers, electric wiring and sockets to structural elements that bear the weight of the building, which include products such as steel and concrete. These inputs are combined to form the finished products or buildings, which are then sold as shown in Figure 7.2. By working on the material inputs, firms add value. To make a profit, the selling price of the finished product must exceed the cost of the material inputs and labour.

However, there are many other costs and expenses that need to be paid for out of the selling price, including interest payments for loans to finance production prior to being paid by the client, investment in plant and machinery

Figure 7.2 Adding value to material inputs

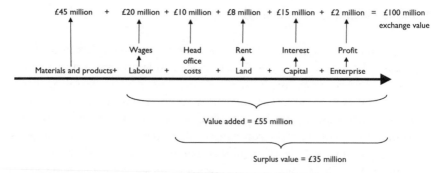

Figure 7.3 Exchange value, value added and surplus value

and rent for the company offices. Profits are the residual after all other costs have been paid. All these expenses come out of value added, making the concept of value added central to the survival of the firm.

The values in Figure 7.3 are for illustrative purposes only. They are not accurate or realistic. Reading from left to right, the production process above the bold horizontal arrow begins with materials and construction products and ends with the rewards to enterprise in the form of a profit of £2 million, assuming materials cost £45 million, wages for labour cost £20 million, head office costs, including bonuses paid to directors and senior staff and the cost of tendering, amount to £10 million, rent for premises is £8 million and interest on loans is £15 million.

Production is the transformation of raw materials into finished goods, representing the output of the combination of materials and labour (which are the direct costs of production). The indirect costs include the head office or cost of administration. The remaining factors of production – land, capital and enterprise – must also be paid for out of sales revenues.

Assuming the selling price of the output is £100 million, if the cost of material inputs is £45 million, then the value added to the materials, shown below the bold arrow, is £55 million: (£100 million – £45 million). If labour wage costs of £20 million are added to the cost of materials, then the total costs thus far are £65 million. If the sales revenues had been £65 million, then there would have been no surplus or residual to pay rent to the firm's landlords, interest to pay for finance or profits to pay shareholders. This residual is called surplus value, which is the amount remaining after materials and labour have been paid. In this example, the surplus value is £35 million.

The key concepts here are value added, surplus value and exchange value. Exchange value is the price agreed between the seller and the buyer, in this case the contractor and the developer. The developer seeks to pay the lowest price to the contractor that the contractor is willing to accept. The contractor seeks to charge the developer the highest price the developer will pay. Often differences and disputes are negotiated, but, if differences cannot be agreed, then disagreements may be resolved through adjudication, arbitration or, as a last resort, the courts.

Value added is the value that contractors add to the basic material inputs by utilizing all other key resources. This is calculated by subtracting the cost of materials from the exchange value, which in this example is £55 million or £100 million less £45 million. As value added is the source of wages and surplus value, the higher the wages bill, the lower the surplus value, as surpluses are available only after wages have been paid. This means that there is always a downward pressure on wages in order to protect the value of the remaining surplus.

As construction labour is fragmented, often working on relatively small sites with a relatively small labour force, this tends to enable contractors to reduce wages in order to remain competitive, or, rather, appear to remain competitive. In reality, because wages are so low, contractors do not have the need to invest in new plant and equipment to make labour more productive, if it is cheaper to employ workers than investing in expensive machinery.

On the other hand, those representing workers seek to raise wages and charge employers what economists call an economic rent. "Economic rent" is the term used to describe a wage above the minimum necessary to keep a worker engaged. This minimum wage is equivalent to what that worker could earn in alternative employment. For example, if a labourer could earn £500 per week as a postman but earns £700 per week as a site labourer, then the economic rent being charged is £200 per week. Even if the wage paid to the construction worker had been £550, it is likely that he or she would have continued to work on site. In this case, the economic rent element of the wage charged would have been £50 of the wage paid per week.

Surplus value is the residual value after material costs and workers' wages, including site labour and managers, plant operators, administrators (including those working in wages departments) and estimators, have all been paid.

They all receive wages for their effort, and only after they have been paid can surplus value be calculated. In this example, the surplus value is £25 million. Once again, surplus value must be shared between a number of key stakeholders, and as a result they come into conflict as part of the nature of the production process. The stakeholders who have to come to some kind of arrangement concerning the distribution of surpluses are the landowners, who receive rent, the financiers, who receive interest, and the shareholders, who receive profits after all other parties have been paid. Because the interest to be paid arises out of past loans for plant and machinery or other expenses in the past, there is little flexibility. Rent must also be paid, as it is essential for the firm to have offices, and possibly storage facilities and warehouses. This leaves profits to be distributed to shareholders, but only after tax is deducted from the remainder. As there is little room for contractors to negotiate other expenses, one of the only ways contractors can retain some profit is at the expense of labour, often poorly represented in the construction industry for the reasons given above. As a result, labour and the owners or shareholders of firms are often in conflict. The higher the wages bill, the lower the profits. Figure 7.4 reveals the production of surpluses. Surpluses are the excess of revenues after material inputs and labour have been paid. If the selling price covers only the cost of materials and the labour used, then there will be no financial resources to pay for anything else and the firm will not be able to survive. Producing surpluses is essential for firms to be able to meet their obligations.

However, what can be clearly seen is that there is significant conflict arising out of the distribution of surpluses between the landlord, the banker and the owner of the firm. In other words, if landlords are seen as landowning capitalists, the banks as financial capitalists and the owner of the firms as industrial capitalists, then it is clear that, although all three are capitalists, there is an inherent conflict between them as they fight for a share of the surplus value produced by labour.

They are all capitalists because they make money by using money. The way they do so varies from one kind of capitalist to the next. Industrial capitalists make money by purchasing materials and transforming them into finished goods. They do this by paying a low price for their inputs and, having added value to them, by selling these inputs for a much higher price. When they purchase their material inputs they want a low price, and when they sell their

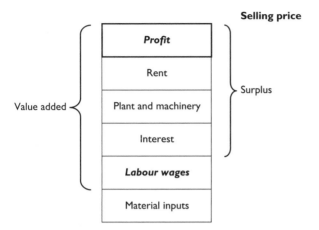

Figure 7.4 The relationship between surplus and value added

output they want a high price. Their objectives are the opposite of those they buy from and those they sell to. Hence a conflict arises. However, the marketplace is a mediator, as the market mechanism is a form of arbitrator for the parties to come to an agreed settlement.

The second type of capitalist is the merchant, who buys materials, warehouses them and sells and distributes them. Merchant capitalists do not transform the materials but simply sell them on at a higher price than they paid for them. Even this adds value to the goods they deal in, because of the convenience and the economies of scale of which they can take advantage. By purchasing in bulk they can receive a quantity discount, which single consumers might not want or need to purchase. In construction, builders' merchants hold stocks of building materials, which small and medium sized firms (SMEs), purchase in small quantities.

Financial capitalists use money to make money by lending money at a rate of interest. They do not usually become involved in the commercial processes. When clients borrow from a bank, various measures are taken by the bank in order to mitigate its risks. Collateral is used in case the project fails, and the bank is then in a position to take legal action to recover the debt. It is also worth noting that builders' merchants are not only merchant capitalists but also banking capitalists for the many SMEs that obtain credit from the builders' merchants. This takes the form of having a "discount" of 5 per cent for immediate payments, no discount for payment in a month's time after purchase and a 5 per cent surcharge in addition for the following month. In effect, the builder's merchant charges its customers a relatively high rate of interest for short-term credit. This may be the only way small building firms can function, and it allows the small firms to work and receive payment before the builders' merchant requires payment.

Concluding remarks

Value added and surplus value explain an important contradiction at the heart of the construction production process. Whenever a number of firms come together to work on a project, there will always be potential for conflict to arise. This is because there is no way of sharing out the value added or the surplus value that will please all the parties. Some will feel they deserve more because they bore the burden of the financial risk. Others will feel they took on a greater share of the work, while others will argue that the value of their input was not reflected in the fees they received. Contracts attempt to meet these claims, but, as circumstances and events on site and during a project are unpredictable, unanticipated and unexpected, disputes will arise between members of the construction team.

8

CONSTRUCTION AND CYCLICALITY

The economic environment is dynamic and ever-changing. Consistent periods of growth or decline are predictable but turning points are difficult to determine with a high degree of accuracy. Economists refer to these significant changes in the economic environment as the business cycle. Economic activity can be measured in terms of a number of variables, including turnover, employment, profits or losses. In terms of the construction industry, the variables used to measure business cycles are generally construction output (see Chapter 2), new orders and employment. The basic business cycle measures variation in activity from quarter to quarter or year to year. A number of business cycles have been identified according to the number of years separating the years of peak activity in the industry, which contrast sharply with construction industry recessions. Recessions in the UK are defined as two or more consecutive quarters of decline in construction activity, utilizing construction output as the measure.

Often business cycles are seen in terms of booms and slumps. However, these booms and slumps are difficult to determine while they are occurring. Economists are always on the lookout for forward-looking indicators to identify turning points. But, in general, the length and breadth of booms, and particularly slumps, are finally determined in hindsight, when analysing the historical data. What we are able to say for certain at any one point in time is that the construction industry, or wider economy, is growing or declining. Output is rarely stable even in the short term, often displaying an upward or downward trend. The key problem for economic forecasters is determining the rate of growth or decline and these turning points. Periods of growth may turn into periods of decline for a variety of reasons: lack of demand arising from market saturation or changes in government policies; oversupply because of investment overestimating future demand or inventory management; and changes in consumption and savings.

A key reason for understanding business cycle fluctuations is to help in mitigating their effects on the firms, the industry and wider economy by anticipating future demand, and supply in particular. Given the negative impacts of recessions on activity, employment and wages, governments may wish to attempt to offset the effect of fluctuations. In the past, governments have often used policies aimed at investing in order to raise demand when demand in the private sector is weak, to try to counter the effects of the business cycle. The success of these counter-cyclical policies is based upon the ability of governments to predict downturns in an industry or the wider economy, then invest to ensure that demand rises or at the very least does not fall by as much as would have otherwise have occurred. This investment tends to be focused towards areas of the economy in which the construction of buildings and structures is needed in the long term, such as transport or energy infrastructure. However, the long time between a downturn starting, determining that there should be an increase in investment and achieving political support for such investment and then the consequent activity actually occurring on the ground, has, in general, meant that such counter-cyclical investment has tended to fail as a political policy.

On average, business cycles in the UK have tended to last between seven and 11 years, which means that the peak of the boom or the nadir of the recession is generally one decade away from the next high or low point, respectively.

The general issues of business cycles are observable in firms' behaviour when there is fluctuating demand in a sector, and the supply response. As a result, it is useful to understand inventory cycles and credit cycles in terms of the cyclical nature of the activity in an economy. Inventories are stocks of goods that are built up when demand is rising and there is a consequent anticipation that it will continue to rise. During growth phases of the business cycle, firms often hire additional staff, invest in additional capital, digitalization, entrepreneurship and managerial skills to produce an output in excess of their sales and store the extra production as stock. This way they can readily supply goods even when demand is increasing, given that expected demand is never entirely predictable and, even if there is an overestimation of expected demand in one month, then sales in future months will use up stock built up previously. However, when firms are clear that demand is no longer rising, they may cut back on hiring additional staff and investing in capital, digitalization, entrepreneurship and managerial skills. Supply is then reduced and firms focus on selling the excess stock to reduce the inventories of goods, which have cost the firm to produce but have, as yet, not earned the firm any income. This behaviour tends to reinforce expanding production during periods of growth and declining production during recessions.

Credit cycles describe periods when borrowing is relatively accessible and interest rates are low, followed by periods when credit is more constrained and interest rates are generally higher. Long-term assets are used as collateral for borrowing purposes, and one of the most common asset types is property. When interest rates are low, asset prices, particularly property prices, increase. Hence, there is interaction between interest rates, borrowing and property prices, as they are all intertwined. Each of the three influences the other two. When property prices decline, it becomes more difficult to borrow, as risk increases and the yield on property increases. The increase in yield increases interest rates, and this in turn reduces demand and prices. Hence, the credit cycle has implications for the valuation of property. When interest rates are low, property prices increase. Therefore, a small change in interest rates may have a major impact on the value of property, even when properties are not necessarily on the market for sale.

Leading indicators are used to predict changes in activity. For example, a rise in construction new orders implies that this will eventually translate into a rise in building output, Lagging indicators imply that employment will increase following a change in housing policy to increase the number of homes being built. Other leading indicators include changes in the level of inventories, changes in GDP and economy-wide employment figures.

Explaining the behaviour of business cycles rests on two economic concepts, the multiplier and the accelerator. Income circulates around the economy. One person's spending is another person's income. Investment in buildings or infrastructure requires finance, which is borrowed. Those who receive an income from the investment spend a proportion of their new income and save the rest. When people spend their income on goods and services, a proportion of their income is passed on to other individuals.

Each time this income is received, some of it is spent and some is saved. The amount of income spent diminishes in each round of spending until the amount is so small as to be of no significance. However, adding up the total income spent in each round results in a larger sum than the original investment. For example, if the initial investment is £100 million and the total spend arising from it as it gets passed around the economy is, say, £240 million, then the value to the economy as a whole is 2.4 times the original investment. This is known as the multiplier effect. Research from LEK Consulting in 2010 indicates that the multiplier for investment in construction in the UK is 2.84. This suggests that, for each £1 spent on construction in the country, the wider economy benefits by £2.84.

The second economic concept is the accelerator principle, or the capital–output ratio. The cost of plant and equipment used by firms is usually greater than the annual output of the goods made with that plant and machinery. For example, plant and machinery may cost, say, £400 million and the annual value of output from that plant may be £200 million. In this example, the capital output ratio is 400/200, or 2.

The economy comprises a consumer goods and services sector and an investment goods sector. Consumer goods are those goods that households buy for their own use or consumption, including food, shelter and clothing, as well as electric goods used in the home. Housing is also a consumer good, although it does share common features with goods in the investment goods sector. Housing is a basic requirement, because of the need for shelter, but it is also an asset, which may generate a rental income or a speculative gain. Investment goods are not goods bought for their own sake. They are bought in order to make money and, ultimately, add to the profits of firms. For example, plant and machinery are used to manufacture products, which are then sold for profit.

Investment can be divided into replacement investment and net investment. When the consumer goods sector is growing, there is a need to replace equipment that is wearing down. This is recognized as depreciation, which is a measure of the capital consumption taking place. Capital consumption uses up the capital equipment or assets until the value of the asset is zero, when it is written off. By setting aside depreciation, firms are able to replace worn-out plant and machinery. If this source of funding were ignored, then after a few years of operation firms would not be able to continue trading, as their plant and equipment would not be able to function reliably and productively. For this reason, firms pass on depreciation as a cost to be borne by their customers. Without the device of depreciation the firm would be subsidizing its customers by not charging them for all the resources, including capital equipment, used up or worn out in the course of manufacturing.

As equipment is constantly in need of repair or replacement if production is to be continued, if the output is the same as previous years, then, if plant is depreciated over a period of five years, each year 20 per cent of the firm's plant needs to be replaced, just to maintain current production capacity. Capacity is a measure of the amount that can be produced using the existing factors of production. If consumer demand increases by 20 per cent, then the firm must invest additional sums to meet the increased output required. In this case, it is equivalent to 20 per cent additional equipment. As 20 per cent of the plant would have been scheduled for replacement, the firm now places an order for 20 per cent additional plant to meet the expanded demand. In other words, it will have to double its annual investment in plant in order to meet an increased demand of 20 per cent. Of course, there are measures the firm can take, if it is not confident that the increase in demand is permanent. It might introduce overtime working, introduce waiting or lead times, sell from stock, buy goods from abroad or choose from the many other options.

However, returning to the firm, if output declines by 20 per cent, then the firm will not need to replace equipment that has reached the end of its working life. In this case, a decline of 20 per cent will lead to a 100 per cent drop in demand for investment goods such as plant and machinery. The investment goods sector is therefore far more volatile than the consumer goods sector. It is this distinction that accounts for the volatility of all economies. When the consumer goods sector is growing, the capital goods sector, including construction, is steady. Each year the construction industry replaces a given quantity of buildings and adds to the stock to meet the increased demand. This additional amount of building is called net investment. Total or gross investment is replacement investment plus net investment. When the economy is growing it requires net investment but when it is declining it does not need to maintain its former level of replacement, although, even during a decline, some replacement investment will still be necessary, or the lower demand for consumer demand could not be met. The business cycle is the result of the interaction of the consumption goods sector and the investment goods sector and depends on the level of confidence that industry and consumers have about the future and their employment and the speculative gain that investors can expect out of their investments.

When investors are confident that the economy will expand, demand is expected to increase. In order to be prepared, investment rises, and this has a self-fulfilling multiplier effect on the economy. This further boosts the economy and forms a virtuous circle of spending and increased investment. Eventually markets become saturated with goods, and, even though demand may not have fallen, the rate of increase declines. This is enough to make demand in the capital goods sector decline, as there is no need for net investment, and, if the decline continues, then replacement investment is no longer necessary and the economy enters a recession.

An alternative approach to analysing business cycles is to adopt a statistical measure, using the approach by Sherman (2014). Using any time series, such as demand or employment or GDP, a cycle is defined as the period from one lower turning point to the next. The cycle base is the average value of the variable during the cycle. This then provides a relative measure of the variance of each point in the time series, using the percentage difference between the average and each point. The variance therefore varies from cycle to cycle, with some cycles exhibiting greater variation than others. The variance gives a measure of the volatility of the variable in any given cycle.

The cycle relative is the variable's percentage of the cycle base at each point in the cycle. Cycle relatives can be indexed and then used to compare cycles. Cycle relatives can also be used to compare the amplitude of cycles.

Cycle amplitude in the expansion phase is the cycle relative at the beginning of the cycle subtracted from the cycle relative at the peak. Similarly, the amplitude of the contraction phase is the cycle relative at the lower turning point minus the cycle relative at the beginning of the cycle, which produces a negative value.

Using this method of measuring business cycles, Burns and Mitchell (1947) describe a full business cycle containing nine stages, from lower turning point to lower turning point, with phase 5 being the upper turning point. Phases 2, 3 and 4 occur in the growth phase and phases 6, 7, and 8 occur during recessions. Sherman (2014) defines the business cycle more broadly, as a period of expansion in economic activity followed by a period of contraction.

Ive and Gruneberg (2000) describe a six-phase construction business cycle, starting at the lower turning point with phase 1, when firms experience growing demand in the form of an increase in the number of tenders they are invited to submit. This phase is followed by phase 2, when labour and material costs begin to increase, forcing contractors to raise their prices. The upper turning point is reached in phase 3, when the market is saturated. Speculative office developments fail to attract tenants due to concerns regarding pricing, and house building slows down in response to rise in house prices, deterring new potential homeowners from entering the market. In the next phase demand and output fall. This leads into phase 5, when recession means that only the strongest firms can survive, with lower profit margins and slower payments causing cash flow difficulties, draining cash reserves and forcing firms out of business. In the final phase, phase 6, the decline in construction work slows down and the remaining firms become busier again; even though the total demand for construction is still very low, the firms still in business find their order books increasing once again. This causes confidence to return to the industry and its clients, and the whole construction cycle starts all over again.

This analysis of construction business cycles implies that the crisis for firms in the business cycle occurs in two phases. First, when the decline in construction demand is approaching the lower turning point, firms are increasingly paid late for work or, in the worst cases, are not paid at all for work they have done, and cash flow difficulties become increasingly frequent in construction, as firms experiencing cash flow issues may not be in a position to enforce contract terms and sue for payment, allowing main contractors to avoid making payments at all. The second crisis point for contractors in the business cycle occurs towards the end of the third phase, when the industry approaches its full capacity, when firms cannot meet their contractual obligations because labour and material resources cannot be found without raising their wages to make projects unprofitable. At this point in the cycle the profits of firms are squeezed, as higher costs cannot be passed on to clients, and many firms may fail at this point even though they may well have orders in hand.

For both these reasons it is often wise to hold cash reserves to enable unexpected cash flow difficulties to be overcome. Such a company strategy is conventionally seen as not making best use of financial assets, as the firm can use its financial assets to generate higher income through investment and trading. Furthermore, substantial cash reserves may not be possible, given the low margins prevalent throughout the construction and, particularly, further down the supply chain, with smaller contractors, where revenue earned on one projects needs to be spent on materials and labour for the next project.

Construction and business cycles

The main determinant of the business models in construction is risk management, pushing risk down the supply chain. The key reason for this is that construction is an inherently risky industry. Activity occurs on bespoke projects that often take years, with profit margins that are low and costs that are difficult to estimate. In addition, these issues are exacerbated by the volatility in demand within the sector. Chapter 1 has highlighted how, whatever people in the economy wish to do, they need construction to have occurred to enable it. This applies to homes to live in, offices, shops and factories to work in, schools and universities to study in and transport, water, energy and internet infrastructure to utilize. The essential nature of construction as a sector that enables the rest of the economy means that it is far more valuable to the economy than just its proportion of GDP would imply. It also means that the construction industry is a bellwether for the economy as a whole, often providing an early sign of an impending recession or a sign of economic optimism and growth. The construction industry is also more volatile than the economy as a whole, and in addition can endure a worse fall in activity than the economy overall.

The financial crisis of 2008 did not impact on all sectors of the UK economy in the same way. Overall, output in the UK economy fell by 6.1 per cent between the first quarter of 2008 and the third quarter of 2009 (see Figure 8.1). Following this fall in output the UK economy recovered, and in 2017 was 10.2 per cent higher than its highest level prior to 2008. However, construction activity was considerably more volatile between 2007 and 2017. This was primarily because construction, as an industry, is particularly reliant on lending from the financial sector, both for the clients and developers wishing to fund projects and the contractors and subcontractors wishing to carry out projects across all sectors.

In contrast to the overall economy, construction output dropped by 17.1 per cent between 2008 and 2009, which was a far greater fall than for the economy as a whole – almost three times the decline. Other sectors of the UK

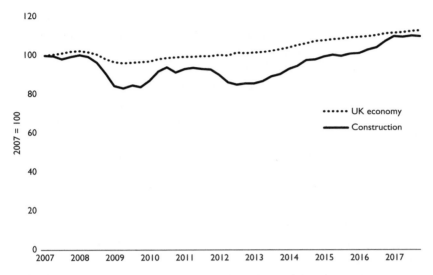

Figure 8.1 The volatility in activity in the UK economy and construction (2007–17)
Source: ONS

economy did not experience as sharp a fall in economic activity. In manufacturing, output fell by 12.5 per cent during the financial crisis, and economic activity in the services sector, which accounts for over three-quarters of the UK economy, fell by only 4.3 per cent between its peak and nadir as a consequence of the crisis.

The impact of the financial crisis on the construction industry also lasted for a longer period of time than in the wider economy. Although the UK economy started to recover from the effects of the financial crisis towards the end of 2009, the construction industry did not experience a sustained recovery in activity until 2012. Initially, following the recession, construction output did temporarily recover in 2009. However, this partial recovery was short-lived, and the construction industry returned to recession as activity fell by two consecutive quarters in 2011. Two consecutive quarters of decline constitute the operative definition of a recession. This phenomenon of a temporary recovery from a prolonged decline is known as a "dead cat bounce", and comes from financial markets, where share prices often experience a short, temporary rise during a downward trend. The underlying, somewhat dark, meaning is that "even a dead cat will bounce" if it is falling quickly and far enough, although the bounce does not represent the health of the cat. It is a vital concept to be aware of and helps to describe the unpredictability of changes in economic growth, which rarely moves in a straight line. As a result, in practical terms it is only with hindsight that it is possible to see the peak or upper turning point of a boom or the nadir or lower turning point of a recession.

Although the construction industry suffered to a greater extent and over a longer period from the financial crisis, it also, eventually, experienced a significant recovery. Between 2012 and 2017 UK construction grew by 29.4 per cent, compared with only 11.3 per cent for the UK economy overall. This is because of the need for construction in the first stage of economic recovery. For example, before manufacturing can take place, factories need to be built, and, although construction investment appears to be very large, the output of the building industry is durable and therefore spread over the life of the building, so not necessarily as high a proportion of costs over time is involved when compared to the annual cost of paying staff employed in the buildings on completion. Nevertheless, it is remarkable to note that construction output in 2017 was 9.6 per cent higher than at the pre-crisis peak of 2008.

Construction cycles and employment

These sharp increases and declines in activity are possible only because of the flexibility of the construction industry. This means that there is a substantial human cost in terms of employment. For this reason, labour is shed each time there is a recession, as the low profit margins mean that firms cannot afford to employ labour that is not productive and not generating an income for the construction firm. This also means that, when a recession impacts on construction, many people leave the industry never to return to it. Figure 8.2 shows that employment in UK construction reached a peak of 2.58 million people in 2008 before falling by 18.7 per cent to 2.1 million in 2013.

Although construction output recovered from 2012, employment in construction did not begin to recover until one year later, in 2013. As a result of the high cost of hiring, training and letting go of employees, even when construction activity begins to rise after the recession firms remained risk-averse,

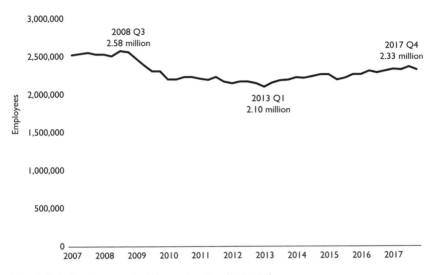

Figure 8.2 Employment in UK construction (2007–17)
Source: ONS

preferring not to start hiring new employees, and instead making the best of the existing numbers employed, until it was necessary to take on more workers in order to fulfil orders. As a result, during the "dead cat bounce" between 2009 and 2011, although the rate of shedding employment slowed considerably, construction firms were not increasing employment because of risk aversion; this turned out to be the correct decision in the circumstances, given that construction output began to fall again after the temporary peak in construction output during 2011.

The sustained recovery in construction employment started in 2013, and by the end of 2017 employment stood at 2.33 million, which was 230,000 higher than at the lower turning point in 2013. However, in spite of this growth, construction employment in 2017 remained 250,000 below the pre-crisis peak in 2008. In effect, the recession in construction had cost the construction industry one quarter of a million construction employees. A proportion of these employees were lost because of early retirement. Some with long experience of the construction industry chose to leave to work in construction industries in other countries where construction activity was still growing, or at the very least appeared to offer more opportunities, as they recovered earlier than the

UK following the financial crisis. Others chose to stay within the UK but to leave the construction industry and work in other sectors of the economy that were impacted less by the financial crisis or that recovered more quickly than the construction industry. Whatever their decisions and destinations, there was less incentive to return to employment in the UK construction industry even if wages were rising.

Not only does employment in construction fall sharply during recessions but the extent to which it falls impacts differently on men and women in the industry, illustrated in Figure 8.3. From the pre-crisis peak of construction employment in 2008 to the nadir of construction employment in 2013, employment of men in construction fell by 17.4 per cent while employment of women fell by 30.6 per cent.

The greater impact on women in construction can be attributed to the gender profile of occupations within the industry. Of the 2.33 million employed in construction in 2017, 2.02 million were male workers and 0.31 million, or 13.1 per cent of the total construction workforce, were women. Within

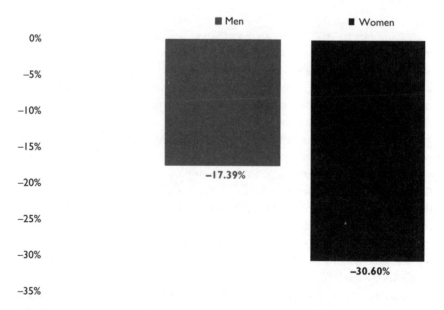

Figure 8.3 The fall in UK construction employment by gender (2008–13)
Source: ONS

this overall figure, there is a stark difference between male and female employment in different occupations, highlighted in Figure 8.4. During the 12 months to September 2017 women accounted for 84.9 per cent of administrative and secretarial occupations in construction, marginally higher than the 82.2 per cent seen ten years earlier. In 2017 women also accounted for 50.6 per cent of sales and other service occupations in construction, compared with 61.7 per cent ten years earlier. These occupations in the industry are often seen as less essential to the business in the short-term compared to managers and directors, operatives and elementary occupations and skilled trade occupations, particularly during a downturn, when the focus is on cost reduction to ensure key operations continue. Figure 8.4 also shows that 98.7 per cent of employees in skilled trade occupations in construction in 2017 were men while 97.2 per cent of construction operatives and elementary occupations in 2017 were men. Men also comprised 84.4 per cent of managers and directors working in the construction industry. In addition, there has been little change over the past ten years.

Costs and behaviour

Capacity is the maximum quantity that a firm and its workers can produce using its plant and machinery. To some extent this is an arbitrary quantity, because it is always possible to work overtime or increase the number of people working, and it is always possible to increase the effort of staff, given the right incentives. From the point of view of an individual construction firm, when the economy begins to slow down, fixed costs per unit of output increase rapidly, because the same fixed cost is spread over fewer sales. Investment plans based on expectations of growth cannot be delivered and the number of units produced actually falls. As the recession goes on, further investment is halted but the number of units begins to fall even more rapidly, and so fixed costs per unit continue to rise, squeezing profits still further as sales continue to decline.

The reverse occurs in the early stages of recovery, as underutilized capital is used up, causing fixed capital costs per unit to fall. However, in this phase of the construction business cycle previous construction product manufacturing capacity may have closed in the meantime and there may be a need to

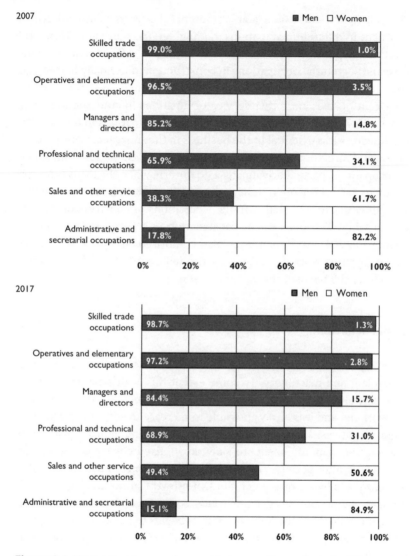

Figure 8.4 UK construction employment by occupation and gender (12 months to September 2007 and September 2017)
Source: ONS

import materials and products in the initial stages of recovery (see Figure 2.6 in Chapter 2).

At the same time, prime costs, which include labour and materials, rise as the market recovers, because increased demand leads to significant labour and materials and product cost inflation, given constrained supply. When demand begins to slow, prime costs per unit may still be rising, as wage growth may have been agreed in the previous year, when demand was still rising, and many materials and products, particularly commodities, may have been bought on futures contracts with hedging to minimize price volatility. Hedging is similar to insuring against losses. By paying for insurance, the value of the probability of the worst scenario is known. If there is no need to claim, the insurance company keeps the insurance premium. Hedging is equivalent to taking out an insurance policy when making a large purchase, whose price can change between ordering and delivery. Commodity prices are determined and traded internationally and their prices are determined by global demand and exchange rates.

In periods of economic growth, the asymmetry in power, whereby main contractors have greater power over subcontractors, begins to change, as subcontractors begin to choose who to work with and at higher wage rates. They may choose not to work with firms with poor records of payment and retentions. This was certainly the case with Carillion, when many firms forced into working for a firm that paid subcontractors in 126 days during the recession chose to reduce their exposure to the company in the year before its liquidation, a period of significant economic growth and a recent peak in construction activity.

The volatility of activity in the construction sector in build to order, or contracting, as it is better known, is partly attributable to the fall in demand. However, the fall in demand occurs in all sectors of the economy during a recession, yet the volatility of construction demand appears to be greater than in other sectors. One reason for this may be the reaction of main contractors to the fall in demand. Given that main contractors primarily win and manage contracts, the number of contracts they have is vital. As demand falls and uncertainty about winning future work increases, given continuing competition from other main contractors, the incentive for contractors bidding for work is to have a lower, sometimes negative, margin on their subcontractors and materials costs. Very low or negative margins are used by contractors to increase their probability of winning a higher proportion of the lower number of contracts coming on to the market. The lower total revenue from these contracts as a whole is sustainable for main contractors only if they extract margin from subcontractors, either by paying them later or keeping a higher proportion of retentions. However, this leads to issues for subcontractors, which tend to be smaller firms, less able to deal with such issues, given their reliance on cash flow and lending. As a consequence, recession alone rarely leads to major contractors going into liquidation. However, the impact on the small and medium-sized enterprises means that the construction industry still loses one-fifth of its workforce in recessions.

Speculative building describes a particular business model within the construction sector, which is defined by the act of building without knowing who the owner of the building will be on completion. The speculative development market operates in a different way from the build to order market, particularly for private house building, which accounts for over 80 per cent of total house building in England. Private house building is the sector of the construction industry that experiences the greatest volatility. Private house builders purchase land with planning permission to build homes or they invest in land without planning permission and apply to local authorities to gain permission to build. House builder revenue is based on the sale of these to potential homeowners. Firms are reliant on lending from the financial sector, including banks and life assurance companies, to invest in the purchase of land. Usually potential homeowners rely on lending from the financial sector to purchase a new home, through a mortgage. This makes the sector particularly susceptible to financial crises, especially the financial crisis of 2008, which was precipitated by defaults on mortgages and issues around mortgage-backed financial securities. As a result, the financial sector was reticent to lend, particularly in areas related to the housing sector. Although there may have been people wishing to buy, without the finance it was largely ineffective demand. Between 2007 and 2009 private housing starts fell by 71.1 per cent in just two years, as a consequence of the collapse in effective demand in the sector (see Figure 8.5). The impact of the financial crisis on the house-building sector was such that, in spite of government policies to incentivize demand and low interest rates to enable demand, private house building in 2017, ten years after the fall in house building began, remained 17 per cent lower than at the pre-crisis peak.

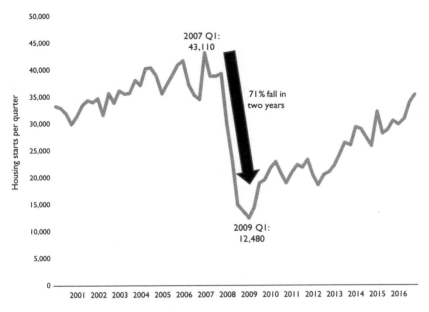

Figure 8.5 Private house building in England (2001–16)
Source: DCLG

Despite the 71.1 per cent fall in demand between 2007 and 2009, not a single major house builder in the UK went into liquidation, as the major house builder business model has developed to deal with this extreme volatility in demand. In order to survive, the business model used by house builders is to push the costs and risk onto the supply chain, subcontracting out the actual construction activity. For example, the annual reports of the UK's top ten house builders by turnover in 2017 illustrate that they directly employed only three people for each home they built across all areas. Unlike the major contractors, major house builders have a key asset, namely an average of five years' worth of land at current building rates with planning permission. In a severe downturn they are able to write down the value of this land in line with the fall in demand, and this provides an asset base from which they are able to recover.

Although major house builders are able to weather the storm, it is quite a different tale for the many SME house builders, which face far greater difficulties in periods of downturn. SME firms often employ directly and so have both high fixed and prime costs. They are reliant upon financial borrowing and previous sales to fund future purchases of land. They do not have a strong asset base of many years' worth of land. As a result, SME house builders are particularly exposed to the impacts of a sharp downturn. The number of SME house builders, building fewer than 100 units per year, reached a peak in 1988, at 12,215 housing units. However, many SME house builders failed during the recession in the early 1990s, and again in the more recent financial crisis. The number of SME house builders in 2016 was just 1,920, 84.3 per cent fewer than at the peak.

It is all too easy to take it for granted that market forces determine the behaviour of firms. While supply and demand are undoubtedly dominant forces at work in the construction market, an important part is also played by the culture and behaviour of individuals and firms. A similar pattern of behaviour spreads across the firms of the industry and affects their performance and permeates throughout the industry, affecting the attitudes of firms throughout the construction sector. Only when buildings fail or major accidents occur are these weaknesses revealed. When short cuts are taken they frequently do not lead to catastrophe, as sufficient safety has been built into the structure, but the lessons are not learned. However, occasionally a disaster takes place and all must pay heed to the dangers exposed. One such disaster was the fire at Grenfell Tower.

CASE STUDY 3: GRENFELL TOWER

The main contractor business model is based around winning and managing projects while subcontracting out risk and activity to a supply chain. However, this means that contractors' focus is on minimizing time and cost on the construction activity, rather than on maximizing quality. In addition, as the activity is subcontracted out to a long supply chain that may differ for every project, there is often a lack of transparency, responsibility and accountability within the construction process.

These issues were highlighted by the fire at the Grenfell Tower, a 24-storey residential tower block, which killed 72 people in June 2017. The tower was purpose-built as an apartment block for social housing in London, but in the aftermath of the fire many issues were raised regarding the refurbishment of the tower. A subsequent independent report on building regulations and fire safety published by the Ministry of Housing, Communities and Local Government (MHCLG) in May 2018, *Building a Safer Future* (Hackitt 2018), states that there were concerns that, not only in the case of Grenfell Tower but in construction more generally, what was initially designed and specified was actually built. The report draws attention to the issue of the quality assurance of the people carrying out the work and the materials used in the construction.

The report highlights that the regulatory system for ensuring fire safety in high-rise and complex buildings was not appropriate. Fire safety protection applied not only in the period when the building was being constructed but also during the entire life cycle of the building, given that it was subject to many refurbishments since the initial construction in 1974. The report also highlights that safety was a problem directly related to the effectiveness of regulators and the culture of the construction industry. It states that the roles and responsibilities for construction and refurbishment across design, construction, maintenance and improvement were not clear. In addition, the report highlights that there were no adequate methods of assessing and ensuring the competence of key people throughout the system. The regulatory system was inadequate, while responsibility and accountability for the construction and refurbishments were dispersed throughout the supply chain.

Although the fire occurred on a social housing building, the issues impacted upon on all towers and other complex buildings. The essential issues of the Grenfell Tower fire apply to construction generally, and the tragedy has the potential to influence and change the way construction occurs as a process.

The fragmentation within the building process is a considerable hindrance to clarity and transparency, responsibility and accountability in the construction industry. The impact of this tragedy is likely to be seen in legal action over the course of years and, potentially, decades as attempts are made to identify those responsible for the lack of safety on the many residential towers and other complex buildings that will need to have work done to redress safety issues.

Over one year after the fire it was still not clear who was responsible; specifiers and designers, contractors, subcontractors, product manufacturers, building inspectors or surveyors? The report highlights that the key driver is to carry out construction activity as quickly and cheaply as possible, rather than focusing on quality. There appeared to be a client focus on price and a contractor focus on ensuring project viability in spite of low or negative margins.

The fragmentation and focus on costs determine the culture within the construction industry, which may well need to change if events such as the fire at Grenfell Tower are to be avoided in future. The different parts of the construction supply chain will have to work collaboratively, to ensure that what is designed and specified is actually built and that changes to the building in terms of maintenance, renovation and refurbishment meet what is designed and specified. What is built, and changes to what is built, need to be fully documented, demonstrating that what was designed and specified is in fact carried out.

Construction new orders and output

Chapter 1 highlighted that activity in the different sectors of the UK construction industry can be measured by the Office for National Statistics construction output statistics. However, the ONS also produces new orders data for some key construction sectors. Whereas construction output measures activity on site in construction, the new orders data measures the contracts signed for construction activity, and, as a consequence, is a leading indicator for construction output. The term "leading indicator" is used to show that the time series may be a helpful indicator of the market or some other variable. For any work to be done, the contract must be signed beforehand, and, if construction demand falls, then it will be seen in a decline in the value and volume of contracts signed before it is visible in construction output.

Construction new orders are likely to be more volatile than construction output, as the contracts, especially for major projects, may be large one-off contracts, and the output for such projects is likely to be spread out over a long period of time. Consequently, construction new orders would be expected to be at a higher level consistently than construction output. However, this is often not the case, because construction activity on a project is not necessarily the same as what was signed up to. There are generally changes in specification during the construction process, either requested by the client or introduced by unforeseen circumstances, such as cost overruns, delays or structural problems in the building or structure. The length of time between construction new orders being signed and the activity on site will vary by construction sector and by project size. The ONS produces construction new orders data for new construction work but not for repair and maintenance sectors. Although repair and maintenance in 2017 accounted for over one-third of construction output (35.4 per cent), it is an aggregation of thousands of small projects across the UK and considerably harder to measure than new construction work.

In private housing, which is the largest single construction market sector, the time, or lag, between new orders and output was estimated to be between three and six months on average, according to the Construction Products Association (CPA) in 2016. As a result, Figure 8.6 illustrates that the private housing output and new orders series both appear to move in a similar manner in most years, and, as expected, the new orders data is more volatile than the construction output series, although only marginally so given that the sector does not generally have large one-off projects that would distort the new orders series. Prior to the financial crisis private housing new orders reached a peak in the second quarter of 2006, while private housing output reached its pre-crisis peak in the fourth quarter of 2006.

The CPA estimated that in the second largest construction sector, commercial, the lag between new orders and output was 12 to 18 months. Figure 8.7 illustrates that declines in commercial output were indicated by declining new orders before output declined. The declines in commercial new orders that precipitated sharp falls in commercial output occurred during periods in which output was still rising towards its peak. This was the case in two recessions in UK construction between 1990 and 2017. In the early 1990s recession, commercial new orders fell sharply from early 1989, yet output only began to fall from the fourth quarter of 1990. During the financial crisis commercial new orders began to fall from 2006, and yet output began to fall only from 2008.

The most volatile new orders are visible in the infrastructure sector, which covers a wide variety of work, from improvement works on roads to, more recently, Crossrail, the largest construction project in Europe by value. Activity in the sector is generally determined by five-year spending plans in regulated

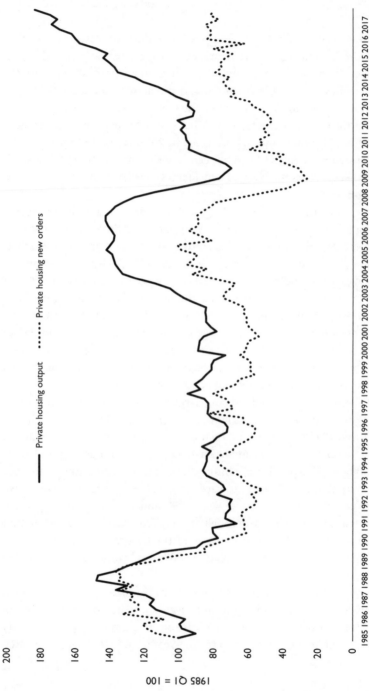

Figure 8.6 UK private housing output and new orders (1985–2017)

Source: ONS

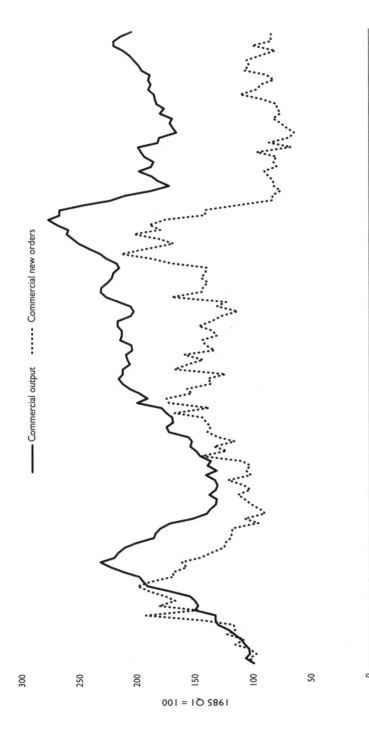

Figure 8.7 UK commercial building output and new orders (1985–2017)

Source: ONS

sectors such as roads, rail, energy and water and sewerage. However, growth in the sector is usually provided by large one-off projects (see Figure 8.8). The early 1990s recession and the financial crisis are not obvious in the chart of infrastructure orders and output, as large infrastructure projects are often signed and on site prior to the economy, and construction, going into recession. Once a project is on site it is unlikely to be cancelled, given the initial costs that have been spent on the long-term project, which would not be recovered if it were cancelled. However, the impact of the recessions on investment in infrastructure are visible as private investment in new projects.

Government austerity programmes implemented following recessions take time to feed through to the data on the infrastructure sector's new orders (see Figure 8.8) from 1993 and again around 2012, after the 1990s recession and financial crisis, respectively. What is clearly visible from the new orders series is when very large one-off contracts are signed, illustrated by spikes in new orders during 1987 and 2017, the activity of which takes years to feed through. These represent major rail projects. In 1987 the key contract for the £4.65 billion Channel Tunnel, the rail line linking Britain and France, was signed. In 2017 the key contract for high speed rail (HS2), the first phase of the £48.5 billion rail line linking London with Birmingham, was signed. The key contracts for the £14.5 billion Crossrail project are less visible, as they occurred over many contracts over a longer period of time. The first key tunnelling contracts for the main works on Crossrail are visible with a small spike in new orders in 2009.

Concluding remarks

Government is the largest client in construction, accounting for over one-quarter of total construction directly as a client. It also influences the construction industry through regulation and the legal framework. This suggests that government could help to soften the impact of the volatility in construction activity by investing counter-cyclically, building when the private sector cannot, particularly as the building and structures it is interested in will be there for the long term; for social housing, education, health and infrastructure. If it invests counter-cyclically, it will be investing at a time of low demand and, as a consequence, will be paying a relatively low price. Unemployment

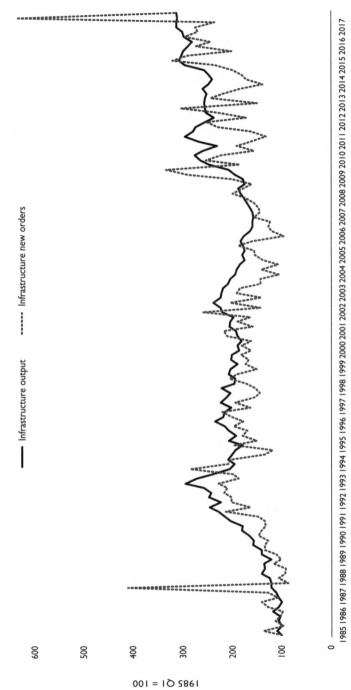

Figure 8.8 UK infrastructure output and new orders (1985–2017)

Source: ONS

represents a total waste of time and human resources. Unemployed people are not productive but they are costly. By creating construction work and employing people who would be otherwise unemployed, there is no opportunity cost. This is a use of the country's resources that would otherwise have nothing to show for their efforts. By building in the public sector they would create a legacy of useful infrastructure, to leave a lasting contribution to help improve productivity and the quality of life in the long term.

If government were to invest in construction at a time of high private sector demand, then government would have to pay a high price, utilizing construction and finance resources at the expense of the private sector, an effect that economists call crowding out. At times of full employment such government interventions have a high opportunity cost. If government cuts its investment in construction at the same time as the private sector, then it exacerbates the impacts of the crisis. This would lead to a loss of employment, skills and capital investment.

If government had long-term coherent and consistent policy objectives in areas where it wishes to have buildings and structures, then it would incentivize construction firms to invest in skills, capacity and technology for the long term, as they would be certain that there would be demand and, consequently, a return on the demand. For instance, if government had a long-term energy strategy and decided that a key part of this was to have nuclear power stations, then firms would invest in nuclear skills and materials and product capacity. However, if government has a record of announcing programmes of investment but with a high degree of uncertainty around the programmes, and has a poor record of policy implementation through changing or cancelling construction projects and programmes, then firms are unlikely to invest, particularly given poor margins.

Government also has a role to play in regulating to ensure good practice within the construction industry. This good practice may take the form of payment terms and retentions that adjust for the asymmetry in power of the main contractors and help subcontractors and the supply chain. Government also has an important role to play in regulating to ensure good practice in terms of safety through building and fire regulations.

9
PROJECTS

Feasibility studies are used to find the economic and financial viability of construction projects, because they are used by decision makers to examine all the cost and revenue implications of proposed schemes. They are systematic and logical and paint a hypothetical scenario of what may happen if the building were to be built. Although they are often used to justify project proposals, they are really only a rational approach to decision making. Feasibility studies are only as good as the assumptions that go into their calculations. They compare all the costs and all the revenues associated with a building proposal and are therefore often called cost–benefit analyses. Cost–benefit analysis allows a systematic approach to comparing the costs with the benefits of the scheme over the predicted life of a project or until it is demolished. Feasibility studies apply as much to private projects built for profit as they do to public sector projects built for the public good.

In construction, a building project can be defined as a development, in which a client engages a contractor to assemble materials and components to create a durable structure, usually on a particular site. The contractor's client is the developer, who brings together the land, assembles the construction team, arranges the finance and takes on the commercial and financial risk for the proposed project. The construction team can include funders, architects, structural engineers, quantity surveyors, building contractors and property or real estate advisors and consultants, as well as the many specialist firms required for their technical skills and know-how. An important element of the whole construction team is the labour force employed by the various participating organizations, whose efforts and skills collectively transform the site and materials into finished buildings.

Each project is discrete: it has a beginning, a middle and an end. One common perception of the construction industry is that it is temporary in nature and employment in the building industry is insecure and irregular. This is not necessarily the case, although it is true that individual workers can find themselves working irregularly, with periods of work followed by periods of unemployment, but – as in every industry – skilled workers find it easier to get work than their less skilled colleagues. It is true that there is little commitment to training the workforce in construction compared to other sectors of the economy, and there is little loyalty in the relations between contractors and those carrying out the work. When work on a project comes to an end, construction firms often lay off their staff if there is no other work for them to do. As we have seen, profit margins in construction are often so low that any profits made by a contractor would quickly evaporate in paying workers when there was no work available.

However, although construction projects themselves are indeed temporary in nature, the construction industry as a whole represents the country's effort invested in the production, maintenance and adaptation of the built environment, and this is a continuing, ongoing and permanent process, necessary for all industrial production, for human well-being, for health and education and for leisure and cultural activities. Because all of society depends on the built environment, the construction industry is a permanent feature of every economy, requiring the workforce to move frequently from one job to another depending on where the work is.

The construction industry can be characterized as the continuous process of bringing temporary teams together to produce and maintain the built environment. These teams of firms vary with each project, because the main contractor needs to engage a specific combination of specialist firms to carry out the work that requires particular skills or equipment. There can be as many as 30 or 40 different specialisms required for any particular project. Specialist firms are required because they provide the pool of skills and machinery that main contractors draw upon as and when required.

This arrangement also suits the specialist firms, as it gives them the opportunity to work for other contractors who require their services, and this helps to give specialist firms some continuity of work. Moving from job to job in this way makes use of specialist labour and machinery across the construction industry as a whole, although it may not always please individual project managers, who cannot avoid delays on their own schemes caused by temporary skills shortages.

Projects are divided into work packages, which define the quantity and scope of work and the materials, skills or technology to be used. Each specialist firm tends to have particular characteristics, such as the size of the firm, the skills and experience of the workforce, their technical knowledge, all of which are needed to contribute to the success of a project. These characteristics give each subcontractor varying degrees of power and influence over the project. This determines the amount of control and negotiating strength each firm has over its part of the construction process and the risks they may take, or, alternatively, offload onto the other firms working on the same project. For this reason it is extremely difficult to ensure that subcontractor firms always work harmoniously together, and disputes are frequent.

They are called subcontractors because the main contractor signs the main contract with the client and then allocates the work packages to the specialist firms as subcontracts. Main contractors are contracted directly by clients, and this relationship forms the interface between the construction industry and the rest of the economy.

Building projects vary depending on how they are organized and on how risk is distributed and managed. Indeed, this is one of the most important considerations of the procurement method or system adopted. Each type of procurement system exposes every participant in the construction process to different levels of risk. Gruneberg and Hughes (2004) suggest that these risks depend in particular on the relationship between the key participants in the procurement system, namely the developer and the main contractor. Procurement systems are general and indicate how power, risk and influence are shared between the various firms involved. The specific relationship between developers and contractors is determined by the construction contract used. Construction contracts cover the following aspects of projects: funding and financial responsibility (to identify who carries the financial burden in the event of project failure); contractor selection (to know the relationship between the contractor and the client and the point in the project when the contractor is engaged); and the type of contract (to assess the extent to which risk and control are organized and distributed in the project team).

In construction, the main role of the main contractor is to manage the process of turning a site into a site with a finished building or structure. To achieve this, the developer signs a contract with a building firm, which undertakes to deliver a finished building. The building firm is seen as the main contractor, whose purpose is to hand over a completed building within an agreed budget. There is usually a warranty period in the contract, following the construction phase, during which some of the agreed contract sum is withheld to ensure that the contractor carries out necessary repairs. Apart from this warranty period to make good any defects or snags, what happens thereafter is not usually the concern of the contractor, on the assumption that the work has been carried out correctly.

The majority of work in the construction industry is based on a variety of contracting arrangements, called procurement routes. Procurement refers to the terms and conditions in a contract for acquiring the services of the various firms needed to deliver a project. A number of established procurement methods exist in construction, going under various headings such as traditional contracting, design and build, construction management, management contracting, and design, build, finance and operate (DBFO). Each of these methods includes a number of variants.

The "traditional" contracting system

The modern "traditional" contracting system emerged in the UK only as a result of the publication of standardized construction contracts by the Joint Contracts Tribunal (JCT) in 1931. At its centre is the JCT Council, which publishes amendments and updates to the contracts.

In traditional contracting the client approaches an architect, who designs the building. One of the time-consuming activities at this early stage is the planning process, and the architect often plays a central role in negotiating with the local authorities and persuading them to grant planning permission. The current procedure is subject to the Town and Country Planning Act 1990. The 1990 Act is complemented by the National Planning Policy Framework, published in 2012, which attempts to simplify planning procedures.

Throughout the design process, building regulations, as defined by the Building Act 1984, also have to be complied with at every stage of the building process. As this implies additional costs to comply with building regulations, a quantity surveyor is usually appointed to estimate the expected cost of constructing the design and to manage compliance with building regulations. The surveyor also helps to draw up the tender documents and contractual terms, and may initiate and manage the tendering process in order to appoint a main contractor to undertake the work.

To begin the process the building work is advertised and contractors are invited to tender. Each potential contractor invited to tender for the work receives a copy of the tender documents, which include drawings of the proposed building and a specification of the construction work, including a bill of quantities, which is a shopping list of the items required and the finishes specified by the architect, making all the tender bids comparable in principle. The tender process is an auction, in which the competing firms offer to undertake the work in return for a given sum of money. The lowest bid usually wins the competition, though not necessarily, depending on the reputation, reliability and ability of the firm and the confidence the developer has in the firm to deliver the required quality for the building. Other considerations may also be taken into account, including provisions regarding environmental impact and local employment and training.

Since their introduction the JCT set of contracts have been the most popular of contracts. Nevertheless, Bowley (1966) points out that the main problem with the JCT contract was that it separated the builder from the design process, making it impossible for the builder to influence the design and specifications before being appointed. As a result, by the time a builder is appointed it is often too late to influence the design, methods of construction and materials used. This is a weakness in the traditional contracting system, as it is the builder who is most familiar with the detailed techniques and technology involved, and the labour-saving and cost-saving methods that might have been adopted had the builder been in a position early enough to influence the project.

Design and build

One method used to overcome these objections to the traditional contract is based on the builder taking on responsibility from the very beginning for both the design and construction of the building. This procurement system, called design and build, can take various forms. For example, some design and build contractors directly employ architects in house. As a result, the firm's architects are familiar with the techniques, experience and ability of the construction workforce. They therefore design accordingly. Alternatively, the contractor may appoint a separate architecture practice to work with the contractor to design the building.

This arrangement reverses the traditional contractual relationship between the architect and the contractor. In traditional contracting the contractor takes instructions from the architect, who has power and control over the builder, because all work has to be approved by the architect and signed off before interim payments can be made to the contractor. In design and build the relationship between the contractor and the architect is more complicated than traditional contracting, as the architect is employed by the contractor. Nevertheless, the architect is professionally responsible for the design being carried out correctly and safely. Naturally, all work must comply with building regulations.

Management contracting and construction management

Two other procurement methods are management contracting and construction management. In management contracting, the management contractor is responsible for managing the contracts signed with the works contractors, which are the firms that actually carry out the work, similar to subcontractors in traditional contracting. The management contractor is also responsible for coordinating the work packages, so that building work can progress smoothly. The contracts are between the work package contractors and the management contractor. This arrangement enables an early start on construction, as contracts can be let by the management contractor as and when they are needed. For example, site clearance and piling contracts can be started even before the design has been completed, enabling the overall duration of a project from start to completion to be shortened. In management contracting, the contractor is also directly concerned with the contractual arrangements, funnelling payments from the developer to the specialist contractors.

In construction management, the contracts are between the developer and the specialist contractors, leaving the construction manager to concentrate on managing the actual construction work. For example, in construction management the client appoints a professional contractor, who then acts as a professional representative on behalf of the client to manage the specialist contractors carrying out the work packages. Construction managers focus on managing the actual work package contractors on behalf of the developer. In construction management, the contracts are placed by the client, and the construction managers are not responsible for payments, only for managing the construction process. In construction management, the construction manager acts as the professional manager of the construction process, appointed mainly to oversee the coordination of the work packages that the specialist firms carry out on site. The construction manager may also advise the developer on technical matters. All communications between the developer and the specialist contractors are transmitted through the construction manager. Thus, in the construction management procurement system the specialist contractors have contracts with the developer or client, not the construction manager, who ensures only that the work is carried out correctly and all firms are paid. In construction management, risk is therefore shared between the developer and the work package contractors, with the construction manager simply overseeing the process on behalf of the developer.

Partnering

Following criticism of the construction industry in the Latham Report (Latham 1994), which describes the construction industry as a litigious, confrontational and uncooperative industry, interest in partnering arrangements increased and attempts were made to introduce partnering contracts to reduce conflict between the various actors in the construction process. The perceived benefit of partnering is that the procurement system could engender trust, cooperation and collaboration to resolve the disputes between all the participating firms and organizations, including the developer, the contractors and their supply chain and those providing finance. Built into the partnering arrangement is a system of regular high-level meetings and dispute resolution procedures, in which senior members of each organization or construction firm meet to settle disputes not resolved by their representatives lower down the management hierarchy, such as site managers. One of the main features of the partnering philosophy is designed to avoid disputes in the first place, with a partnering arrangement designed to be non-confrontational.

A family of contracts was devised by David Mosey, called project partnering contracts (PPC 2000) and term partnering contracts (TPC 2005), revised in 2008, and these have been used on a number of large projects in both the public and private sectors. A similar set of contracts first published in 1993, called the new engineering contract (NEC), adopts a similar approach to PPC 2000 and emphasizes dispute resolution, and they are also very widely used. The latest version of the NEC is the NEC4, published in 2017, which makes some minor changes to the NEC3, mainly in the terminology used. When the 2012 London Olympic Games were constructed the NEC3 was used, and this example will be discussed in more detail in the next chapter.

The Private Finance Initiative

One system that came to the fore in the 1980s and 1990s was a procurement route that encouraged large construction firms to extend the service they offered to clients in the public sector. This method involved the contractor not only constructing the building but also retaining ownership for a period of time, ranging from 15 to 30 years, at the end of which the building or infrastructure asset could be transferred to the public sector.

These projects were called public–private partnerships (PPPs) and came under the terms of the Private Finance Initiative (PFI). The PFI enabled the government to acquire schools, hospitals, infrastructure such as bridges and roads and other facilities by using the financial resources of the private banking system to fund projects rather than taking on loans directly. As the collateral for the finance was embedded in the built assets themselves, it was argued that government could avoid adding the borrowing to the national debt. This was known as off-balance-sheet borrowing, and was not included in the national debt. The traditional method of financing infrastructure or public housing was to borrow money from the market by issuing government bonds. Government bonds are promises to repay a sum of money at a given date in the future in return for a fixed annual rate of interest. The national debt is the total of all public sector borrowing using bonds and equivalent financial instruments.

The PFI offered (and continues to offer) an alternative method of financing public sector projects because PFI contracts legally commit the public sector to guarantee a flow of cash in the future to pay for the use of the facilities for a known number of years. At the same time, the public sector has the reassurance that the buildings will be fit for purpose and well built, as the construction firm retains responsibility for the quality of the buildings. Unfortunately, it became apparent that the overall cost of PFI projects was so much greater than conventional procurement methods that the PFI system gradually fell out of favour, and its use declined. Moreover, many of the projects, such as prisons, schools and hospitals, could not fail or go bankrupt as they were essential public sector provisions. As a result, when projects ran smoothly they generated profits for the contractors, but if they ran into financial difficulties the public sector was obliged to step in. This meant an unequal distribution of risk, which economists call moral hazard. Moral hazard allows individuals to lay a bet that, if it wins, they collect the prize but, if they lose the bet, then someone else must take the consequences. This moral hazard applies to public sector PFI buildings such as hospitals, schools and prisons, when there is a social and political need as well as the economic benefit of the facilities. They could not be closed down because of the financial difficulties of a supplier. The public sector has no choice but to intervene to keep the facilities operating.

Nevertheless, PFI obliged contractors and funders to consider the life cycle costs of projects taking into account not only the cost of construction but also the annual cost in use, including the cost of maintenance and other running costs, as long as the building remained functional. Effectively, the PFI made it necessary to carry out a feasibility study of each project in an attempt to demonstrate that the proposed project was financially and economically viable.

Speculative building

Not all construction work is carried out using contracting. Much building work is speculative building, such as the majority of house building, which was 43 per cent of all UK construction output in 2017, according to the ONS (2018a). This occurs when a building firm purchases a site and constructs a building without necessarily knowing who the final purchaser of the build-ing may be. This is most common in house building but offices, commercial premises and general warehousing and factory units may also be built spec-ulatively. If this is the case, the construction firm acts as a speculative builder and takes on the additional risk of not realizing a profit from the sale of the building on completion. Usually this speculative risk element is taken on by a developer acting as a client of the contractor rather than the building firm itself. Normally the profit margins of contractors are so low on building pro-jects that it is unusual for construction firms to generate sufficient funds to undertake projects speculatively.

Of course, notwithstanding the above about contract builders and spec-ulative builders in general, there are many variants of these two types for organizing construction projects. Indeed, all projects are unique in one way or another, as there are always features in every project that require special atten-tion, including unique geological problems, one-off design features, technical innovations or particular contractual conditions.

Feasibility studies

Regardless of whether a project is carried out on a speculative basis or built to contract, one of the most effective ways of justifying a building proposal to funders, politicians and local people is to argue that the benefits of the project are greater than the cost of the scheme. For this reason, feasibility studies are often referred to as cost–benefit analyses. Even before developers instruct their quantity surveyors to prepare tender documents, projects are assessed for their potential financial and economic viability. Financial viability refers to the flows of money in a project, including the cost of land, the cost of construction and the cost of finance, as well as the revenues from rent and the sale of the property. There are, of course, many costs and revenues that do not translate into cash. For example, there are the costs of disruption, the loss of amenity and even the loss of jobs caused by some projects, as well as the gains to the community by the creation of new amenities, increased ser-vices and the increase in property values as a result of new buildings in the neighbourhood. These non-financial costs and benefits should also be taken into account, even though they may be difficult to measure, controversial and disputed. Financial viability takes into account only the flows of cash. Economic viability includes both the financial and non-financial costs and benefits, namely those costs and benefits not actually paid by the developer. In the language of cost–benefit analysis, financial costs and benefits are referred to as tangible costs and benefits, and the non-financial costs and benefits are called intangible costs.

If a project is not viable, then changes are necessary to ensure that the revenues from the sale or rent of the completed building or structure are greater than the total costs. Feasibility studies examine all the costs and benefits arising out of the project. A cost is a sacrifice and a benefit is a gain. Costs and benefits are therefore distributed between all the participants and stakeholders affected by the project and those who stand to gain. For a project to be viable, the value of the gains must be greater than the value of the costs.

It is perfectly possible for a project to be financially viable but not economically viable. This would occur, for example, if a project generated large profits but also led to major environmental damage, such as the pollution of a river over a wide area, affecting many lives. An example of such a disaster (with the benefit of hindsight) was the Bhopal chemical plant disaster and pollution in India, which killed and caused so much suffering to thousands of families in 1984 and since then. Bowonder (1987) demonstrates how it is not possible to anticipate all the problems that can arise. Carrying out a feasibility study will not alter anything. Nevertheless, the Bhopal disaster and the 2011 Fukushima nuclear power station disaster in Japan make it reasonable for feasibility studies to take into account the scale of the potential risk of such events occurring. This applies equally to the recent Grenfell Tower fire in London. These failures highlight the need to manage risk and allow for the cost of risk mitigation even at the feasibility study stage. This is one of the many factors that need to be taken into account early on in many projects. The appeal of feasibility studies is that they enable a number of elements, such as the cost of the site, construction costs, annual repair and maintenance budgets over the life of the building, energy costs and all forms of revenue and risk, to be considered in a systematic way and the relative importance of each to be taken into account, measured and assessed.

Feasibility studies take into account the whole building life cycle, from the construction phase and the building-in-use phase to the demolition or dismantling phase. Although the dismantling phase may become particularly important and significant in considering the decommissioning costs of nuclear power stations, it is also worth noting demolition costs and issues with the trend towards very high-rise buildings in tight city centre sites.

However, there are a number of criticisms of the concept of cost–benefit analysis. There are usually disagreements about the value to attach to various items. There is often an optimism bias, as cost–benefit studies are used to justify projects for which clients require financing. As well as there being disputes over the values of particular costs and benefits, it is also difficult to establish agreement over the distribution of costs and benefits. Their values are difficult to assess, and intangible costs and benefits are often little more than arbitrary guesswork. For example, the value of a benefit may differ between a wealthy individual and someone living in relative poverty. There is no method for attributing values to costs and benefits consistently. The valuation of a benefit may be understated while the valuation of a cost may be exaggerated, or, indeed, vice versa. The distribution of costs such as noise and pollution, which may adversely affect a large number of people, needs to be compared to the value of the benefits to a few, or even one individual. One might ask the question: is a gain of £1 million to one individual equivalent to a £1 cost to each of 1 million people? Problems such as this invariably occur in discussions about the validity of feasibility studies and can lead to disputes and disagreements.

Feasibility studies compare the costs and benefits arising out of a proposal. They ask the question: what do the benefits need to be worth in order to make a project worthwhile? For example, in Figure 9.1 the costs over the life of a building are £1 million. If the total value of benefits is only £0.8 million, then the benefits need to be revalued and the costs reduced for the project to go ahead. If the new values are not acceptable, then the project proposal should be rejected. Which benefits can be increased and which costs can be decreased to make the project worthwhile? For example, it may be a block of flats, and the additional value of each flat may need to be increased by 25 per cent. If the revaluation of the costs and benefits are not acceptable to the developer's decision makers, then some other benefit increase or cost reduction must be found. Otherwise, the project should not go ahead. The feasibility study is only a tool to help decision makers by making them aware of the cost implications of their decision and the issues that may follow.

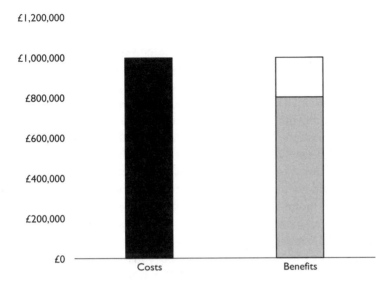

Figure 9.1 The feasibility study: finding the missing value

The values given to intangible costs and benefits are only quantitative esti-mates made to weight arguments for and against projects. Often values are implicit in how we behave, and sometimes the values we place on some build-ings include the implicit value of an amenity. For example, house values in the catchment area of a good school reveal how much parents value giving their children an excellent education. This is an example of the intangible benefits of building a school. Apart from price, products invariably embody several features that encourage consumers to purchase them, such as comfort and design, status and image, taste and culture, convenience and time saving. This also often applies to buildings when there is a speculative element to be taken into account. Otherwise, only the cheapest product or service would be purchased every time. The term used for this phenomenon of taking several attractive features into account when marketing a product such as a new car or building is "hedonic pricing". Hedonic pricing takes into account the fact that the reasons for making a decision are complicated, and no one reason is usually sufficient for reaching a decision. Design, convenience, cost saving, prestige, image and time saving are all examples of the many factors that need to be taken into account in the decision-making process.

Time value of money

Because of the durability of buildings, there are often several years between buying or constructing a building and receiving a profit from it. The question is: if you were to invest a sum of money, would you be satisfied if you received the same amount back in, say, two years' time? The incentive to invest is receiving a return on your investment. That return must compensate you not only for taking a risk on the investment but also for the fact that you have delayed spending that amount on consumption. The minimum rate of return on the amount you invest is your time value of money. If the rate of return were lower, you would not invest, and any greater return would be a bonus.

The time value of money reflects the notion that money today is worth more than the same amount in the future. This is because money today can be spent, or invested, immediately but holding the same amount of money for a future purchase carries many risks. The money may lose value because of inflation, the product or service may no longer be available in the future or new competition to purchase the object may increase its price. To attract a purchaser, a discounted offer is needed.

Because the sum invested has to be set against future revenues, and future revenues are spread over a large number of years, all cash values need to be valued at one point in time; this is usually the present year, but sometimes a year in the future may be selected. If all valuations are not based at the same moment, they cannot be compared or combined, as they are not consistent.

The distribution of costs and benefits

Major construction projects impact on different people. These people are often referred to as stakeholders. Stakeholders may be the developers or those living in the neighbourhood of the development, or those gaining from the increase in employment or even those losing their livelihoods as a result of the project. While some stakeholders may benefit, others may lose. It is quite common for those harmed by a development to be vociferous in their objections, while those who benefit are restrained, not wishing to advertise their gains, and remain silent. Indeed, many of those who benefit may not even be aware that they will benefit before they actually make use of the facilities, such as a new motorway, whereas those whose homes need to be demolished to make way for the new road will make a determined effort to object to planning consent, as is their democratic right.

From an economic point of view, feasibility studies attempt to assess the distribution of costs and the distribution of benefits between the many stakeholders in an attempt to apply utilitarian principles. Utilitarianism can be summarized as the greatest happiness of the greatest number. Although this appears to be a fair and reasonable approach, it is extremely difficult, if not impossible, to apply in practice.

First of all, the value we attach to things depends on our subjective opinions, our income and whether or not we are receiving a benefit or paying a cost. How much we value things depends on how strongly we feel. Just as two people receiving the same type of flu vaccination will experience different levels of pain, the actual measurement of the intensity of the psychological pain experienced by one person cannot be verified or compared with that experienced by another person. When a project has an impact on those in the vicinity, such as replacing a rural environment with a housing development, the loss of amenity to a wealthy family may be valued more highly and require a greater amount in compensation (even though they may not even spend the money) than the same loss of amenity to a poor family, for whom a small amount of compensation would make a considerable difference to their quality of life. No single valuation can be applied to all. Finally, when evaluating a cost the value attached tends to be greater if the stakeholders expect to receive compensation compared to the value they would have to pay if they had to pay compensation. Various techniques have been developed to overcome these difficulties, but in all cases it is not possible to achieve universal agreement.

Applying utilitarian principles to feasibility studies implies that the total value of all gains to those benefiting from a scheme must be greater than the total losses to the losers. However, this may lead to an unsatisfactory conclusion if, for example, 999,999 people each lose £1 while a single developer gains £1 million. Nor is it possible to say with certainty that the value of the subjective gains is greater than the total value of the subjective losses. For this reason, Vilfredo Pareto came to the conclusion that, as one cannot be certain that the gains are greater than the losses to the losers, a project should not go ahead if there are any losers. The concept of Pareto optimality means that one is in an optimal situation if it is not possible to change anything without harming anybody. This implies that the status quo is to be preferred if there are any negative impacts on some stakeholders. In fact, Pareto's criterion would prevent so much necessary development that projects invariably go ahead even though they are in a Pareto-suboptimal situation.

Decision criteria

Given the test of Pareto optimality, a number of investment criteria have been devised to aid decision makers. The criteria include the payback period, the internal rate of return, the net present value, the benefit–cost ratio and the maximum negative cash flow. They each shed light on different aspects of a project, and it is certainly not sufficient to make decisions on the basis of the investment criteria alone. Judgement is always required.

The payback period is perhaps the simplest investment decision tool to explain. If a project costs £100 million and earns £25 million in profits from rent, then the building will have paid for itself in four years. This is a measure of the risk that, in purely cash flow terms, the investor is exposed to losing money for a limited period of time. However, it says nothing about the durability of the building. If the building were no longer usable after the fourth year, then it is possible that an alternative structure might have been able to offer a longer life and greater returns in the longer term.

The internal rate of return is equivalent to the rate of interest paid by a bank. In other words, if a project costs £10 million and the annual revenues less the annual costs are £1 million per year, then the internal rate of return is 10 per cent, or £1 million divided by £10 million. If the internal rate of return is greater than the interest rate paid to borrow funds for the project, then the project will be able to afford the loan and pay it back. The higher the rate of return, the lower the risk of defaulting on the loan. However, the weakness of the internal rate of return is that, when it is used to compare two investment proposals, the higher rate of return may be smaller in money terms than the alternative project, and the profit to be made is smaller as a result.

The net discounted present value is the present value of all the future revenues less the total costs of the project over its life. It is because the costs have been deducted that we refer to this criterion as the net present value. This shows the increase in the asset value of a firm as a result of the decision to invest in a project, even before it has been built, as its immediate worth is the value of the net discounted present value. To find the net discounted present value we must now turn to discounting.

Discounting

At the heart of any feasibility study is the arithmetic of calculating the total gains and costs over the life of a building to establish that the gains are greater than the costs. If the costs are greater than the benefits, then the implied decision is to reject the proposal. All the costs and benefits are modelled over the life of the project, from construction through to demolition, or possibly until there is a change of use. As buildings are durable, feasibility studies set out in a table the total costs and revenues for each year over the life of the building. This can be seen in Table 9.1. In years 1 and 2 the annual expenditure on the building under construction is £8 million in both years. Thereafter the annual running costs are shown as £1 million until the final year, when £3 million is invested to prepare the building for sale. In the third column from the left are annual revenues, which do not appear until the

Table 9.1 The discounted cash flow

Year	Annual cost £ million	Annual revenue £ million	Net annual benefit £ million	5%	10%	15%	20%
1	£8	0	−£8	−7.62	−7.27	−6.96	−6.67
2	£8	0	−£8	−7.26	−6.61	−6.05	−5.56
3	£1	£2	£1	0.86	0.75	0.66	0.58
4	£1	£2	£1	0.82	0.68	0.57	0.48
5	£1	£2	£1	0.78	0.62	0.50	0.40
6	£1	£2	£1	0.75	0.56	0.43	0.33
7	£1	£2	£1	0.71	0.51	0.38	0.28
8	£1	£2	£1	0.68	0.47	0.33	0.23
9	£1	£2	£1	0.64	0.42	0.28	0.19
10	£3	£33	£30	18.42	11.57	7.42	4.85
		Net present value		8.79	1.71	−2.44	−4.87

third year, when the building is expected to generate an income of £2 million per annum until year 10, when it is sold for £32 million and rental income is valued at only £1 million (not shown in the table). The net annual benefit is the difference between the annual revenues from all sources and the annual running costs.

The remaining part of Table 9.1 is concerned with aligning all the costs and revenues to find total costs and revenues by discounting the annual figures. It can be seen in the table that the higher the discount rate, the more rapidly annual values decline as time passes. This means that, when interest rates are high, future revenues are less significant than when interest rates are low. Discounting is the inverse of compounding. Just as interest is compounded into the future to evaluate a future sum of capital including interest, future sums of money, including interest payments, are discounted back to the present. Simple interest is when interest is paid on a sum of money called the principal. If the principal is £100 and the rate of interest is 10 per cent, then simple interest is £10 per year. This remains at £10 each year for the duration of the loan. With compound interest, not only does the original £100 earn interest but, in the second year, the interest earned in the first year, £10, is added to the principal of £100 to become the new principal of £110. The interest on the new principal in the second year is £10 plus £1, which is added to the value of £110 at the end of the first year, which makes £121 at the end of the second year.

In the first year the total amount including compound interest is calculated as in Equation 9.1:

£100 + £100 × 0.1 = £100 + £10 = £110   Equation 9.1

Note that £110 = 100 × (1 + 0.1)   Equation 9.2

Therefore, in the second year this becomes

£110 + £110 × 0.1 = £100 (1 + 0.1)(1 + 0.1)   Equation 9.3

The right hand of the equation is £110 × (1 + 0.1),
which equals £121   Equation 9.4

as £100 × (1 + 0.1) = 110, which, if multiplied
by (1 + 0.1), equals £121   Equation 9.5

In other words, the original sum is multiplied by (1 + r) for each year that passes, squared in the second year, cubed in the third year, and so on. The equation for compound interest is

$$FV = PV(1+r)^i$$ Equation 9.6

where

FV = future value
PV = present value
r = rate of interest
i = number of years

If compounding takes us into the future, then simply rearranging Equation 9.6 allows us to move from the future back to the present. To find the present value, the formula for discounting a future sum is given by Equation 9.7 and can be applied to as many years as required

$$PV = FV \times \frac{1}{(1+r)^i}$$ Equation 9.7

Equation 9.7 is used in feasibility studies to calculate the present value of a future sum of money for each year in the life of the building. This is necessary in order to find the total of all the annual net revenues.

Armed with the discounted cash flow table and the graph, Figure 9.2, showing the internal rate of return (IR), the net discounted present value and the internal rate of return can be assessed. In Table 9.1 the net present value declines in value as the discount rate increases, which can also be seen in Figure 9.2. The significance of this trend curve is that the internal rate of return is where the curve crosses the horizontal axis, namely where the discounted revenues are exactly equal to the discounted costs. It should also be noted that the net value of the project depends on the discount rate used. Some companies use a target rate of discount that all projects must satisfy

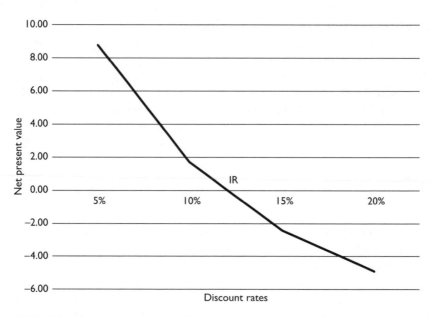

Figure 9.2 Estimating the internal rate of return from the discounted cash flow table

before projects are even considered. The main point of the internal rate of return is that it must be greater than the cost of borrowing or the project will not cover all its costs.

The benefit–cost ratio shows the relative size of benefits to costs. The greater this ratio is, the more benefits are generated per pound invested. The maximum negative cash flow is a key tool of management, as it shows not only the size of the greatest deficit in the project but also when that deficit is likely to occur. This shows how much the developer requires to borrow when the project is most in need of financing. This is achieved by examining the net cumulative cash flow, which is shown schematically in Figure 9.3. It can be seen that the greatest negative cash flow occurs in year 2, when the greatest amount outstanding is –£17 million before revenue begins to come in to the project. The cost of the land, construction and interest payments all have to be paid before revenues begin to reduce the size of borrowing. In this simplified hypothetical example, the maximum negative cash flow occurs in year 2, and only in year 10 does the project cash flow become positive.

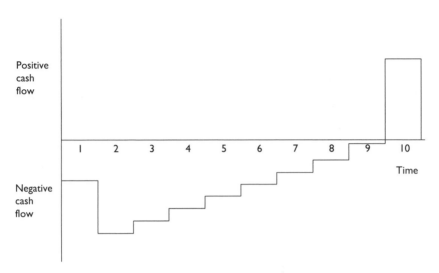

Figure 9.3 The net cumulative cash flow of a project

Choosing the most appropriate financial criterion can also lead to disagreements. Some use the rate of return, which is the value of the return divided by the capital employed or invested. Although the rate of return can be a useful indicator, it tends to favour smaller projects. The main use of the rate of return is to compare it to the rate of interest the developers pay for financing the project. The rate of return must exceed the interest rate. The net discounted present value is the aggregated annual value of benefits less the aggregated annual value of costs. This represents how much the assets of the developer increase as a result of the successful outcome of the investment. Another important investment criterion is the maximum negative cash flow. This is the value of the deficit when more money will have been spent than at any other time. This mostly occurs during the construction phase. This sum must be covered by the funding and finance when the amounts outstanding are at their greatest. If insufficient sums are available, the project comes to a halt and the survival of the developer would be endangered. Perhaps the most commonly used investment criterion is the payback period. Unfortunately, it may be the most common, but it can also be misleading. This criterion gives the number of years it would take to recover the investment. Although this is a useful measure of exposure to risk, it favours short-term investments over projects designed to be durable.

Site acquisition

Before any construction project can be considered, the site where the building will stand needs to be acquired. This is often done by purchasing an option on a site. Options give the developer the right to own or develop a site for a limited period of time at the end of which the site must be purchased or the right to build on it forfeited. The developer must use this time to propose a use for the site and have a design drawn up to win planning permission and financial backing. Once planning permission is granted, contractors and their supply chain can be appointed and contracts awarded. At this point construction firms then move onto the site to demolish existing structures, if any, and prepare the site for the new building work to take place.

Meanwhile, the ownership of the site is transferred to the developer, who must transfer funds for the purchase of the land. As large sums are involved, the developer requires finance for the purchase, and the daily cost of interest on the loan can be extremely costly. This places a great deal of pressure on the developer and all those involved on the project to complete the project as soon as possible to limit the cost of finance, which depends on how long it takes to repay the loan. This underpins the pace of work on site and adds to the stress, pressure and disputes when delays occur.

On completion, the building may be used for its planned purpose, sold or rented out. Often completed developments remain empty or void for a period, adding to the cost of borrowing to finance the project. The length of the void period is one of the major risks faced by speculative developers, who build without necessarily knowing who will eventually occupy the completed building, such as office developments or residential dwellings. Although the contractors' work may come to an end, they may still have responsibilities for making good faults or snags and other work, depending on the contract terms.

The construction sector mainly delivers one-off bespoke projects. As a result, every building is unique. This is because the combination of the features of buildings is always unique in terms of the geological conditions of the site, the function of the building (residential, commercial, health care, education, etc.), the architectural design and the types of materials used in the construction. Each building is also unique in terms of its location relative to other buildings and facilities, such as shops, schools and hospitals, and even bus stops and stations for ease of access to work.

This one-off nature of the construction sector distinguishes it from other sectors of the economy, which produce many identical products or services. In general economic theory, textbooks suggest that in manufacturing, for example, managers may decide the quantity to produce or the unit price of their products in order to maximize their company's profits. We have seen, in an earlier chapter, that economic theory proposes that, in order to maximize profits, it is necessary, in principle, to estimate the level of output that equates the marginal cost and the marginal revenue. In other words, at every level of output, the question is: what is the addition to total cost of producing one more unit and what is the addition to total revenue that it would bring in? The profit-maximizing level of output is the one at which the marginal cost is equal to the marginal revenue. Once this level of output is known, the decision maker can produce that output and, arguably, obtain the highest level of profits, on the assumption that the quantity produced can be sold. This assumes that the manager of the firm is in a position to decide how much to produce.

This is not the case in construction. In practice, manufacturing firms often deliberately produce additional units beyond what they expect to sell in order to hold back some products as stock in reserve in case of an unexpected surge in demand. Producing for stock also enables manufacturers to smooth production, rather than constantly needing to adjust their output to meet orders. In construction, contractors produce to order. Only speculative developers are in a position to select a quantity of buildings that best meets their own needs. For example, speculative house builders decide how many houses to build on a given site, although that decision still has to comply with planning permission.

The key point is that standard economic theory assumes that the production manager is in control of output decisions and uses that control to determine how much to produce. However, this is not the case in construction contracting. In construction projects the contractor does not have the freedom to decide how much to produce, except the decision to take on the project or not. The size of a project is determined by the client and the planning permission granted and each project's technical requirements. The decision on the size of a building project is beyond the control of the construction contractors and does not depend on the size of project that would optimize the contractor's profits.

The needs and preferences of the contractor are rarely, if ever, taken into account during the early stages of a project, when feasibility studies are carried out. It is assumed that the purpose of the building and its commercial success depend on its function and the demand for the finished building. Contractors are assumed to be willing to undertake the work, as they knowingly calculate the cost of construction and add a profit margin in their tender bids. As contractors are not given the opportunity to decide the most efficient size of building from their own point of view, it should not be surprising that building firms do not always compare favourably with firms in other industries in terms of efficiency and productivity.

As discussed in an earlier chapter, firms in the construction industry tender for work. Often this is based on a fixed tender price. As soon as contractors are selected to carry out the building work, their strategy for managing the building project is to reduce their costs as much as they can in order to increase the profit margin. Before they are appointed, main contractors base their tender prices on the costs submitted by their own subcontractors and suppliers, and only once they know their own costs do they add a margin for profit. After they are appointed, they are in a much stronger position to increase that profit margin by going back to their suppliers and asking them to lower their prices (a Dutch auction). This occurs because, when main contractors are in possession of a contract, they are empowered with the knowledge that they can actually offer work to their subcontractors.

Concluding remarks

Shen *et al.* (2010) examined 87 feasibility studies of construction projects in mainland China. They found that there was far more interest in economic and financial criteria than in social and environmental considerations. They felt that feasibility studies are important in influencing the behaviour of developers and the practice of construction, but did not provide any justification for this view. They also saw corporate social responsibility as being a key driver of good sustainable practice but did not give reasons for the poor performance of social and environmental attributes used in feasibility studies in practice.

Feasibility studies are often conducted by developers because it is a requirement of the legislation or the planners. The main motive of developers is to use any given site to generate profitable returns. However, the public sector has a responsibility towards third parties affected by developments to safeguard their interests at the same time. This could lead to an example of market failure, as the general public is rarely organized to object to developments that are harmful to their interests. In recognition of the weakness of third parties, Shen *et al.* (2010) advocate government intervention to protect the environment through environmental policies and legislation and administrative approval, though these are not specified. They also propose that developers should collaborate with government offices, urban planners, architects and engineers at the feasibility study stage. However, they do not say how this collaboration would produce more sustainable development. In economic terms, each stakeholder has a unique rationale for participating in a project. Each requires an income from the project. This focuses on short-term gains rather than delaying returns or passing them on to future generations, sacrificing them in the near term. Unless feasibility studies recognize the economics of development and meet the interests of the participants, the results of the feasibility study are likely to be ignored. Although Shen *et al.* discuss the situation in China, the issues raised are of more general and international relevance.

10

THE ECONOMICS OF CONSTRUCTION PROJECT MANAGEMENT

In most factories, offices and shops the same workforce provides the same product or service every day and occupies the same work space, where they can be found and contacted. However, in construction, as work proceeds, the labour force is not fixed. Different groups of subcontracted labour may come together for only one project and then move on to work in new locations. Moreover, specialist firms may be present on site only for relatively short periods, as long as their services are required. These constant changes of work locations and people lead to increased supervisory and management costs and can reduce productivity, often unavoidably.

Often the technical problems on site mean that the workforce has to learn on the job and adjust to the new work environment very quickly, making it difficult to take advantage of all the technical skills and experience they may have. As every project is unique in one way or another, it is always necessary to adapt to the particular circumstances and problems thrown up by the introduction of new methods or materials or plant and machinery. For example, when a new material or building product system is introduced, it will have an impact on some other parts of the building process and the labour force, who are tasked with the job of integrating the new product or method with existing building methods and materials.

Construction project management is, therefore, more challenging and complicated than management in other industries, made even more challenging for project managers by very low profit margins, which imply that any errors of management can remove the little profit margin the firm might achieve not only on a project but also for the contracting firm, as the low profit margins in construction make it very difficult to make up for the losses on individual projects by increasing the price on other projects. If one project loses £1 million and the firm's profit margins are only 2 per cent, then the firm would have to increase turnover by £50 million to make up for the loss, by either increasing prices or winning a great deal of work, just to make up for the losses on one project. Moreover, as all firms attempt to lower their costs below those estimated during the tender process, they are continually seeking to cut corners and take short cuts, leaving few opportunities for further cost reductions. They adopt cost-cutting strategies because of the low profit margins needed to win in the tendering process, and, as a result, the level of trust within the construction team can be low.

Another reason project management in construction is extremely difficult is because each project means assembling a new team of people from several different companies, most of whom have never worked with their new colleagues before. Their individual strengths and weaknesses can be learned only as the project develops, making it likely that productivity will tend to be low to begin with, albeit improving as time passes and the workforce learns to work together. Because of subcontracting, the project manager is more remote from the people who actually undertake the work on site than would be the case if they were employed directly. Subcontracting stretches the lines of communication and reduces the authority of site managers, often leading to disputes between firms, each with their own workforces. By outsourcing almost all work to subcontractors that are specialist firms, monitoring costs, supervising work and evaluating building quality becomes a complex management task. It is, therefore, the nature of the contract arrangements themselves that creates some of the difficulties faced by construction project managers and their site managers.

Managing construction: the London Olympics

From a construction project management point of view, the London Olympics in 2012 was a series of separate but linked projects. The link between the projects was the Olympic Delivery Authority (ODA), supported by the delivery partner, CLM, which was a consortium or joint venture of three large construction firms, namely CH2M Hill (renamed CH2M), Laing O'Rourke and

Mace, set up to oversee the construction of the games as a whole. The role of the ODA was to act as the client that all projects had in common. As the client, the ODA and its delivery partner were in a position to oversee the contribution of each of the main contractors, subcontractors, sub-subcontractors and suppliers in all the projects of the London Olympic programme. With their bird's-eye view of all their projects, the aim of this arrangement was to place the ODA and CLM in a position to coordinate the activities and anticipate problems and difficulties before they were able to cause delays or additional costs.

Because the construction industry is a project-orientated industry, in which one-off buildings or structures are assembled, each project can be distinguished in terms of the combination of its size, function, design and location. Similarly, the contractual arrangements are also tailored to meet the needs of each project, depending on the relationship, attitudes and circumstances of particular clients. One of the main aims of project management is the management of risk, especially financial risk. The financial strength of each firm within a project impacts on its ability to take on risk, making it necessary to match firms to their work packages in a way they can manage the cash flow. Cash flow is key to the survival of the firm, by ensuring that receipts from sales or loans from all projects flow into the firm at a faster rate than the outflow of cash. The cash flow of each project can affect the survival of the whole firm and its suppliers, and this can have a domino effect on other firms, in turn affecting other projects where the subcontractors may be working. A company failure, arising out of cash flow difficulties during a project, can have consequences affecting other subcontractors and can add delays and costs to a number of otherwise unrelated projects.

Every contractor has a portfolio of projects. Within each firm individual projects affect and are impacted by the other projects in the portfolio. It is as if each project has to compete for attention and a share of the firm's resources. Construction project management is concerned with every aspect of managing construction work before, during and following operations on site. This includes defining the scope of the project, which may involve dealing with site preparation, technical and managerial issues, design issues, sustainability issues, construction waste management, facilities management, building maintenance and the end-of-life demolition. The main objectives of managing construction projects include controlling costs, ensuring timely delivery and providing buildings and structures that meet the quality and safety required by clients.

Construction project management begins even before a project begins to take shape on a building site. In the tendering process contractors have to assess the project from a project management point of view. They need to assess the methods of construction to be adopted (depending on the design), the resources required and the costs involved. There is a need for each firm to assess how the project will fit in with its other projects and commitments in terms of timing and cash flow. For example, if a firm has three projects, it has to consider if it can carry out the work on the third project before it has been paid for the first one – or will the capital outlay be too great to manage comfortably, even if the work has been carried out successfully? To cover such a situation, contractors need cash or liquid reserves to tide them over until they are paid. There is a need to assess the cash flow implications of a firm taking on more work than it can afford if it impacts on the firm's cash flow and liquidity reserves. As we have seen in the previous chapter, due to the low profit margins in construction, if a firm loses £2 million on one project, it may need to undertake £50 million of work just to restore its revenues and profits to their previous position.

Very large projects are often too big for one firm to take on alone, as the financial risks may indicate predictable cash flow problems while waiting for payment from the client. For this reason, contractors frequently form themselves into consortia, as with CLM in the case of the London Olympics. A consortium may comprise a small number of contractors sharing the project and spreading the risk.

In construction, relationships between the management and workforce of main contractors and subcontractors tend to last, at best, for the duration of a project. This means that there is little time to communicate an understanding of the client's requirements and priorities. Moreover, clients may have more complex requirements than simply setting objectives in terms of cost, time and quality alone. Other factors may also need to be taken into account, including health and safety considerations, skill training, environmental and sustainability issues and the impact of a project on the local community.

With a view to avoiding bottlenecks and delays, the client requires information about the other work commitments of the main contractors and their subcontractors bidding for the work. If delays on a project are to be avoided, then the total work commitments of all firms in the supply chain need to be assessed, including their work commitments on other projects. Otherwise, hold-ups caused by the outside workload may cause delays. Ideally, by coordinating work across different projects that the main and subcontractors may be working on, progress can be monitored and possible bottlenecks can be identified in good time to avoid delays, but this rarely if ever happens, though something approaching this was achieved during the London Olympics. This monitoring means that, instead of working in silos, the workload of all the subcontractors can be coordinated to everybody's benefit.

Of course, at the time of bidding for work many firms do not know whether they will have the work they expect, and nor are firms in a position to predict the duration of their work on other sites. There are many uncertainties facing every firm about to embark on a project. For example, according to Rimmer (2009), main contractors may offload risk and responsibilities onto subcontractors without necessarily informing the client, making it impossible for the client to control the management process or monitor the cost, timing and quality of the work. Nevertheless, continuous client engagement with the construction process is important. Otherwise, avoidable changes can occur that could have a negative impact on a project.

Having won a contract, the management of risk by the main contractor is partly achieved through subcontracting. As subcontractors are employed to carry out work packages, the role of the main contractor diminishes. Indeed, subcontractors may also employ sub-subcontractors to undertake parts of the work package, and in the process the main contractor is further removed from the workforce. This enables the main contractor to offload some of the risk onto the specialist firms carrying out the work, some of whom may be small firms with only a small workforce or gang of workers.

Managing a project also means managing a client, and this implies that the client remains fully informed about progress, issues and methods in order to lead the project. If the client does not take the lead role, the contractor or the architect may have to assume the leadership role, and they may not carry out the project in line with the needs of the client. Therefore, to avoid disappointment and the unexpected, there needs to be a continuous dialogue between the client and the building team to enable the client to remain fully informed and legally responsible for decision making, if not in control in practice.

Project management in construction is more complex than in other industries because main contractors are appointed to deliver a finished building, but they do so by ordering materials, hiring plant and subcontracting the work to a number of specialist contractors. In general, a supply chain may consist of a main contractor, subcontractors, materials and building component suppliers and plant hire firms. Mead and Gruneberg (2013) describe the London Olympics supply chain as consisting of tiers of firms. Tier 1 contractors were the main project contractors. Tier 2 were the groundwork contractors, tier 3 the plant providers and tiers 4 and 5 the plant maintenance firms and parts suppliers, respectively. Each firm in the supply chain had its own supply chain to meet its requirements.

As every contractor working on a project has its own portfolio of projects, a delay on a relatively small subcontracting contract for an outside project can have major consequences if, for example, it causes a delay because a large package of work cannot be started, leading to a chain reaction of hold-ups. Without detailed knowledge of the workload of all the firms in a supply chain, it is not possible to plan construction progress with any confidence. The client is in a position to obtain the necessary information by making transparency a condition of tendering.

Before transparency can occur in the supply chain, there is a need to build trust. Loosemore (2006), for example, suggests that managing risk requires communication, transparency and the involvement in the decision-making processes of all firms in the supply chain. Building a rapport between the members of the supply chain needs to extend beyond the construction phase and on-site activities to include the environmental, social and political requirements of projects.

From the outset it is useful to communicate a vision for the project from the client's point of view, in order to convey the aims and ambitions for the project to the different contractors who ultimately deliver the construction work. This vision then defines the critical success factors, such as improving customer satisfaction and delivering the requirements cost effectively. Other aspects of the project may include the manner in which the project is conducted and other priorities the client may have regarding quality, sustainability, dispute resolution, the conditions of employment, the training of labour and the treatment of subcontractors by main contractors.

These issues were dealt with on the 2012 Olympics programme using a balanced scorecard or weighted importance rating system. The scorecard lists various priorities of the projects, including the timing and build quality, and also the manner in which the construction work is to be carried out, such as timely payments to subcontractors. Each criterion is then given a weighting; the higher the weighting, the more important the criterion is as far as the client is concerned.

The scorecard acts in two ways. First, it is a management device, used to award marks, say out of ten, for the degree to which the client's priorities have been met in the tender documents of each bidding firm. Second, marks out of 100 show the relative importance of each priority, because not all priorities are equally important to the client. The priorities are placed in order of importance and the most important priority or objective is given a value of 100. The second most important priority is then given a weighting relative to the first priority, say 80, and so on. The balance in the balanced scorecard refers to the weighting that each priority is given. Aggregating the total weighted score of each priority enables the tenders to be compared.

A simplified scorecard is shown in Table 10.1. Four criteria for selecting the client and setting out the priorities of the project are given at the head of each column: cost, timely delivery, quality and health and safety. These priorities are given weighting depending on the decision maker's judgement of their relative importance. Under each weighted heading are the specific attributes of the work that need to be defined and delivered. As part of the tender documentation, all the contractors in the tendering process submit a description of how they intend to carry out each aspect of the work. Each attribute is then assessed according to how it is seen as meeting the requirements of each criterion, and this assessment is given a mark. Each mark is multiplied by the weighting for that particular priority. All the weighted scores are then given an aggregated score, which is the balanced scorecard assessed value of each contractor's tender. In this way the contractors tendering for the work demonstrate to the client how they intend to deliver each aspect of the work.

These priorities and objectives are discussed when firms tender for the work, but after a project has been awarded these commitments are often ignored, forgotten or paid only lip service. However, if the tender documents and discussions at the tender stage make it clear that the winning firm's performance will be measured and monitored by the client not only during the construction phase but also after completion of the building work, the firm's work will be compared to its undertakings made during the bidding process to form part of the contract to meet a variety of requirements as the project

Table 10.1 A simplified balanced scorecard

Cost	Timely delivery	Quality	Health and safety
Project	Meeting deadline	Function	Scope
Materials and	Project scheduling	Design	Construction
components	Work package	Workmanship	on site
Contract	integration		Behaviour

progresses. Contractors can then be held to account. This is one of the main reasons for using a balanced scorecard.

Defining the critical success factors in the balanced scorecard and how they can be measured sets a wider agenda for each project than simply completing the building on time, with quality and to budget. The balanced scorecard can be helpful in communicating what the client expects from the main contractors and their subcontractors. Moreover, the client's requirements need to be budgeted, and this whole process of setting objectives and budgeting accordingly reduces the likelihood of disappointment later on. With the addition of so many possible objectives it is important to resolve contradictory objectives, which could lead to confusion, such as asking for a commitment to training while seeking construction cost reductions.

Since their introduction in 1998 key performance indicators (KPIs) have been an attempt to measure aspects of UK construction industry performance. The KPIs continue to be published by both Glenigan and Constructing Excellence, and are included in the construction statistics published by the Office for National Statistics. KPIs cover a range of issues, including satisfaction from the different perspectives of clients and contractors, building defects, the predictability of costs, profitability, productivity and safety.

In order to persuade a number of contractors to bid competitively for the work, a developer needs to attract contractors to bid. To generate interest among potential contractors, some effort may be needed to interest potential contractors. Just because a firm may have sufficient construction capacity – labour and resources – to undertake the work does not mean it will necessarily bid for the work. There are several options that might be used to create interest in a project. For example, according to Mead and Gruneberg (2013), a number of methods of engaging with main contractors and their supply chains were used to attract contractors to bid for work in the 2012 Olympic Games in London.

Mead and Gruneberg (2013) describe one-way and two-way discussions with possible suppliers. One-way discussions were used to inform the supply chain of the developers' plans; for example, events were organized that potential firms were invited to attend. Two-way discussions were similar to market sounding exercises, actively seeking feedback from suppliers on the technicalities and practicalities of proposals. The purpose of these events was to create interest among specialist firms, inform potential participants of the engagement process and make contact with other members of the supply chain.

From the developer's point of view, early discussions with the supply side help to establish the extent to which capacity exists in terms of the skills and resources needed to meet the needs of the proposed project, and even to assess the market conditions in each specialist market. They are also useful for assessing an individual firm's ability to undertake the work. According to Mead and Gruneberg (2013), a relatively low risk ratio of the value of any one contract to total turnover is approximately 25 per cent of total turnover, and certainly no more than 30 per cent. The difficulty with these figures is that they assume that the firm is financially robust. When Carillion went into liquidation in 2018, this ratio would not have prevented or revealed the collapse of the company and its construction arm.

Nevertheless, the more a contractor's output is concentrated in one project, the more vulnerable the contractor is to the vagaries of adverse conditions arising in that project. Risk of default is always present in construction, and due diligence or the checking of the financial solvency and strength of firms needs to be carried out by examining the accounts of contractors. The ratios of most interest include liquidity ratios, gearing ratios, performance ratios and profit ratios, which can be found in any accountancy textbook. Together, these ratios provide an indication of the strength of a firm.

Liquidity ratios compare the assets of a firm to its liabilities. To be solvent, a firm must have more assets than liabilities. Therefore, the ratio of assets to liabilities needs to be greater than one. However, there are times when firms such as developers invest in their own expansion by borrowing, and on those occasions their liabilities may be greater than their assets, at least until the building project is successfully completed. In those cases, the ratio of assets to liabilities would be less than one, and the firm would be technically insolvent. In such a case, the reason for the technical insolvency should be clearly identifiable in the form of a major investment that has not yet matured into making a return to the firm.

Building information modelling

Construction project management is always changing and evolving as new procurement systems are introduced, new types of contracts are used and methods of managing projects are adapted to take advantage of new technology. Currently major changes are taking place in managing projects with the application of computer power to integrate the management of projects.

According to the National BIM Standard – United States (2017), building information modelling is the application of information technology to facilitate construction management processes from design and construction to maintenance. As firms adapt to the new technology, it remains impossible to predict how firms will actually make use of the new methods offered by BIM. Several attempts have been made to predict the use of BIM but the reality is that firms will use the technology when it is in their interests and will refrain from using it if they find that it interferes with their profitability and control over their own businesses.

As in all construction projects, BIM involves collaboration between all the parties engaged in the delivery of a building or structure. One of the distinguishing features of BIM is that it gives an opportunity to every participant in the construction team to engage with the project before construction begins by creating a virtual environment as the design develops. According to Glick and Guggemos (2009), this approach to the building process encourages firms to work closely together by adopting integrated project delivery (IPD). IPD brings together construction managers, the skilled trades, off-site fabricators, suppliers and construction product manufacturers. This virtual environment vertically integrates the staff of independent firms working together with a view to improving the efficiency of the construction process, from design to demolition. Firms can contribute to projects by exchanging information through the virtual model developed online to reduce waste and improve efficiency.

However, this requires both a willingness to share information and a degree of trust between the firms in the project team, which does not always exist.

BIM is simply a management tool. It has potential benefits but it also includes potential risks. On projects for which several firms are expected to work together, it may not always be possible to coordinate construction activities. We have seen in earlier chapters how conflict is always present in any production process, and construction sites are ideal breeding grounds for disputes. Moreover, BIM relies on all participants being able to use and apply the technology. If one or more firms in the construction team are unable to use BIM software, refuse to collaborate or fail to work with the other subcontractors because of lack of trust, expertise, knowledge or experience of BIM, then the benefits of using BIM can be lost.

Ku and Taiebat (2011) have identified the following barriers to implementing BIM. First, there was at the time of writing a lack of skilled personnel able to operate BIM software. They have also found that the cost of implementing BIM is prohibitive for many small firms, which also leads the larger firms to feel reluctant to introduce a new method that would be expensive for other construction team members to implement. In the early days of BIM there was a lack of understanding of the collaborative application of BIM and how each firm might insert its contribution to the model. It was also seen as difficult to work together using BIM techniques, because the legal requirements and contractual arrangements were not sufficiently defined. Since 2011 these difficulties have begun to be resolved.

Nevertheless, problems and difficulties remain, especially when something goes wrong. Design entails copyright issues, and, as Azhar, Khalfan and Maqsood (2012) point out, it is not always clear who owns the design when a variety of firms have contributed inputs into the design. Apart from legal and organizational difficulties, Ku and Talebat (2011) also identify the additional costs involved in working with BIM before staff are fully trained, experienced or conversant with BIM, and a reluctance on the part of some participants to engage fully with BIM, whereby some firms adopt a culture of inflexible and defensive working practices. The cost of training in the use of BIM is a further barrier to its widespread application. Over time, no doubt, these obstacles to the implementation of BIM will gradually disappear, but it is always the case with change brought about by new technology that there are early adopters with other firms eventually following.

Although there are many legal and organizational obstacles to be overcome, there is little doubt that, as a new generation of senior managers take up positions of responsibility, the enhanced use of computing power is likely to continue in construction, along with other rapidly developing techniques such as 3D printing, the use of drones and robots on building sites and the internet of things. It is unlikely there will ever be a time when change and innovation in construction cease.

Concluding remarks

A number of economic characteristics of working on building sites impede productivity in the construction industry. For example, the use of subcontracting work on site means that those responsible for managing the process and instructing labour have little direct control over the workforce, because construction labour is employed by the subcontractor, not the main contractor. Another example of a characteristic of the construction industry that leads to problems is the temporary nature of construction teams, which are put together only as each project comes on site. As a result, when projects are started, those actually carrying out the work are not necessarily known to the managers on site. Their strengths and weaknesses are not known, and they may be asked to carry out work they are not familiar with.

Nevertheless, construction managers overcome these practical difficulties on a daily basis, although not without cost, as the data shows that productivity in construction is invariably lower than in other sectors of the economy. This is not to say that construction is always a poorly performing industry. Many of the problems in construction can be overcome, especially on large projects that last several years. For example, during the construction of the London Olympics a number of effective management techniques were adopted, which enabled the buildings for the games to be built on time, to a high standard and on budget, and without any fatalities – a factor that often mars the achievement of building major construction projects throughout the world.

BIBLIOGRAPHY

Abdel-Wahab, M. & B. Vogl 2011. "Trends of productivity growth in the construction industry across Europe, US and Japan". *Construction Management and Economics* 29(6), 635–44.

Acharya, N., Y. Lee & H. Im 2006. "Conflicting factors in construction projects: Korean perspective". *Journal of Engineering, Construction and Architectural Management* 13(6), 543–66.

Azhar, S., M. Khalfan & T. Maqsood 2012. "Building information modeling (BIM): now and beyond". *Australasian Journal of Construction Economics and Building* 12(4), 15–28.

Baiden, B., A. Price & A. Dainty 2006. "The extent of team integration within construction projects". *International Journal of Project Management* 24(1), 13–23.

Barney, J. 1991. "Firm resources and sustained competitive advantage". *Journal of Management* 17(1), 99–120.

Barougha, A., M. Shoubia & M. Skardib 2012. "Application of game theory approach in solving the construction project conflicts". *Procedia: Social and Behavioral Sciences* 58, 1586–93.

BEIS 2018. *Monthly Statistics of Building Materials and Components: April 2018.* London: Department for Business, Energy and Industrial Strategy.

Bidarianzadeh, G. & C. Fortune 2002. "Lean thinking and the delivery of sustainable construction projects". In D. Greenwood (ed.), *Proceedings of the 18th Annual ARCOM Conference 2–4 September 2002, University of Northumbria*, vol. 2, 567–76. Reading: Association of Researchers in Construction Management.

Bowley, M. 1966. *The British Building Industry.* Cambridge: Cambridge University Press.

Bowonder, B. 1987. "An analysis of the Bhopal accident: project appraisal". *Industrial Hazard Management* 2(3), 157–68.

Bresnan, M. & N. Marshall 1999. "Achieving customer satisfaction? Client–contractor collaboration in the UK construction industry". In P. Bowen & R. Hindle (eds.), *Proceedings of the CIB W65/W55 Joint Triennial Symposium: A Focus for Research and Practice in Construction, Cape Town, 5–10 September*, 256–64. Delft: International Council for Research and Innovation in Building and Construction.

Build UK & CECA 2018. Action to Support Carillion Workers and Suppliers, press release, 17 January. London: Civil Engineering Contractors Association. Available at:

www.ceca.co.uk/media/295137/ceca-and-build-uk-press-release-action-to-support-carillion-workers-and-suppliers-immed-17-january-2018.pdf (last accessed 1 January 2018).

Burns, A. & W. Mitchell 1947. "Measuring business cycles". *Science and Society* 11(2), 192–5.

Capen, E., R. Clapp & W. Campbell 1971. "Competitive bidding in high-risk situations". *Journal of Petroleum Technology* 23(6), 641–53.

Carillion 2017. *Making Tomorrow a Better Place: Carillion Annual Report and Accounts 2016*. Wolverhampton: Carillion.

Chan, P. 2002. "Factors affecting labour productivity in the construction industry". In D. Greenwood (ed.), *Proceedings of the 18th Annual ARCOM Conference 2–4 September 2002, University of Northumbria*, vol. 2, 771–80. Reading: Association of Researchers in Construction Management.

Chang, C. & G. Ive 2007. "Reversal of bargaining power in construction projects: meaning, existence and implications". *Construction Management and Economics* 25(8), 845–55.

Dainty, A., S. Millett & G. Briscoe 2001. "New perspectives on construction supply chain integration". *Supply Chain Management* 6(4), 163–73.

De Valence, G. (ed.) 2015. *Modern Construction Economics: Theory and Application*. Abingdon: Routledge.

Delmar, F., A. McKelvie & K. Wennberg 2013. "Untangling the relationships among growth, profitability and survival in new firms". *Technovation* 33(8/9), 276–91.

Department of Veterans Affairs 2017. *VA BIM Standard: BIM Manual V2.2*. Washington, DC: Department of Veterans Affairs. Available at: www.wbdg.org/FFC/VA/VABIM/bim_manual_2017.pdf (last accessed 1 July 2018).

Durdyev, S. & J. Mbachu 2011. "On-site labour productivity of New Zealand construction industry: key constraints and improvement measures". *Construction Economics and Building* 11(3), 18–33.

Eastman, C., P. Teicholz, R. Sacks & K. Liston 2011. *BIM Handbook: A Guide to Building Information Modeling for Owners, Managers, Designers, Engineers, and Contractors*, 2nd edn. Hoboken, NJ: Wiley.

Engwell, M. & A. Jerbrant 2003. "The resource allocation syndrome: the prime challenge of multi-project management?" *International Journal of Project Management* 21(6), 403–9.

Gambatese, J. & M. Hallowell 2011. "Factors that influence the development and diffusion of technical innovations in the construction industry". *Construction Management and Economics* 29(4), 507–17.

Glick, S. & A. Guggemos 2009. "IPD and BIM: benefits and opportunities for regulatory agencies". Available at: http://ascpro0.ascweb.org/archives/2009/CPGT172002009.pdf (last accessed 1 July 2018).

Global Construction Review 2018. "Digital diggers". 6 August.

Glyn, A. 2004. "The corn model, gluts and surplus value", Department of Economics Discussion Paper no. 194. Oxford: University of Oxford. Available at: www.economics.ox.ac.uk/materials/working_papers/paper194.pdf (last accessed 1 July 2018).

Green, B. 2017. *Productivity in Construction: Creating a Framework for the Industry to Thrive*. London: Chartered Institute of Building.

Griffiths, A. & S. Wall 1999. *Applied Economics*, 8th edn. Harlow: Longman.

Gruneberg, S. & W. Hughes 2004. "Analysing the types of procurement used in the UK: a comparison of two data sets". *Journal of Financial Management of Property and Construction* 9(2), 65–74.

Gruneberg, S & G. Ive 2000. *The Economics of the Modern Construction Firm*. Basingstoke: Palgrave Macmillan.

Gruneberg, S. & I. Murdoch 2011. "Specialist contractors' views: testing the NSCC State of Trade Quarterly Report results against market conditions". In C. Egbu & E. Lou (eds.), *Proceedings of the 27th Annual ARCOM Conference*, 505–12. Reading: Association of Researchers in Construction Management.

Hackitt, J. 2018. *Building a Safer Future – Independent Review of Building Regulations and Fire Safety: Final Report*. London: Ministry of Housing, Communities and Local Government. Available at: https://assets.publishing.service.gov.uk/government/uploads/system/uploads/attachment_data/file/707785/Building_a_Safer_Future_-_web.pdf (last accessed 1 May 2018).

HM Government 2017. *Industrial Strategy: Building a Britain Fit for the Future*. London: Department for Business, Energy and Industrial Strategy.

Hughes, W., P. Hillebrandt & J. Murdoch 2000. "The impact of contract duration on the cost of cash retention". *Construction Management and Economics* 18(1), 11–14.

Ive, G. & S. Gruneberg 2000. *The Economics of the Modern Construction Sector*. Basingstoke: Palgrave Macmillan.

Jergeas, G. 2009. "Improving construction productivity on Alberta Oil and Gas Capital Projects". Paper presented at annual conference of Construction Owners Association of Alberta, Edmonton, 21 May.

Kadir, M., W. Lee, M. Jaafar, S. Sapuan & A. Ali 2005. "Factors affecting construction labour productivity for Malaysian residential projects". *Structural Survey* 23(1), 42–54.

Kiyotaki, N. & J. Moore 1995. "Credit Cycles", Working Paper no. 5083. Cambridge, MA: National Bureau of Economic Research. Available at: www.nber.org/papers/w5083.pdf (last accessed 1 July 2018).

Koskela, L. 1997. "Lean production in construction". In L. Alarcón (ed.), *Lean Construction*, 1–10. Rotterdam: Balkema.

Kotler, P., G. Armstrong, J. Saunders & V. Wong (eds.) 1996. *Principles of Marketing*. Hemel Hempstead: Prentice Hall.

Ku, K. & M. Taiebat 2011. "BIM experiences and expectations: the constructor's perspective". *International Journal of Construction Education and Research* 7(3), 175–97.

Latham, M. 1994. *Constructing the Team: Final Report of the Government/Industry Review of Procurement and Contractual Arrangements in the UK Construction Industry*. London: HMSO.

Loosemore, M. 2006. "Managing project risks". In S. Pryke & H. Smyth (eds.), *The Management of Complex Projects: A Relationship Approach*, 187–204. Oxford: Blackwell.

Loosemore, M. 2014. "Improving construction productivity: a subcontractor's perspective". *Engineering, Construction and Architectural Management* 21(3), 245–60.

Mead, J. & S. Gruneberg 2013. *Programme Procurement in Construction: Learning from London 2012*. Chichester: Wiley.

Morris, P. 2010. "Research and the future of project management". *International Journal of Managing Projects in Business* 3(1), 139–46.

Mott, G. 1993. *Accounting for Non-Accountants: A Manual for Managers and Students*, 4th edn. London: Pan Books.

Nash, J. 1951. "Non-cooperative games". *Annals of Mathematics*, second series 54(2), 286–95.

Nason, R. & J. Wiklund 2018. "An assessment of resource-based theorizing on firm growth and suggestions for the future". *Journal of Management* 44(1), 32–60.

National Institute of Building Sciences 2017. "About the national BIM standard – United States", 4 July. Available at: www.nationalbimstandard.org/about (last accessed 1 July 2018).

Office for National Statistics 2017a. *United Kingdom National Accounts: The Blue Book 2017*. London: ONS.

Office for National Statistics 2017b. *Annual Business Survey, UK Non-Financial Business Economy: 2016 Provisional Results*. London: ONS. Available at: www.ons.gov.uk/businessindustryandtrade/business/businessservices/bulletins/uknonfinancialbusinesseconomy/2016provisionalresults (last accessed 1 May 2018).

Office for National Statistics 2018a. *Construction Output in Great Britain: December 2017*. London: ONS. Available at: www.ons.gov.uk/releases/construction outputingreatbritaindec2017andocttodec2017 (last accessed 1 August 2018).

Office for National Statistics 2018b. "Employment by industry". London: ONS. Available at: www.ons.gov.uk/employmentandlabourmarket/peopleinwork/employmentandemployeetypes/datasets/employmentbyindustryemp13 (last accessed 1 August 2018).

Office for National Statistics 2018c. "Gross fixed capital formation, by sector and asset". London: ONS. Available at: www.ons.gov.uk/economy/grossdomesticproductgdp/datasets/grossfixedcapitalformationbysectorandasset (last accessed 1 June 2018).

Office for National Statistics n.d. "Annual population survey: estimates for employment by industry and occupation in the UK". London: ONS.

Oke, A. & P. Ogunmola 2014. "Retention bond and performance of construction projects in Nigeria". *Journal of Construction Project Management and Innovation* 4(1), 721–33.

Penrose, E. 1959. *The Theory of the Growth of the Firm*. New York: Wiley.

Pettinger, R. 1996. *Measuring Business and Managerial Performance*. London: Pearson.

Quirke, J. 2018a. "Project management robot". *Global Construction Review*, 22 February.

Quirke, J. 2018b. "German firm invents scaffolding robot". *Global Construction Review*, 10 April.

Quirke, J. 2018c. "Off-grid people pod". *Global Construction Review*, 30 July.

Ramachandra, T., J. Rotimi & K. Hyde 2015. "Causes of payment delays and losses in the construction industry". *Construction Economics and Building* 15(1), 43–55.

Ramsden, P. 1998. *The Essentials of Management Ratios*. Aldershot: Gower Publishing.

Raworth, K. 2017. *Doughnut Economics: Seven Ways to Think Like a 21st-Century Economist*. London: Random House.

Reddy, K. 2011. *BIM for Building Owners and Developers: Making a Business Case for Using BIM on Projects*. Hoboken, NJ: Wiley.

Ricardo, D. 1817. *On the Principles of Political Economy and Taxation*. London: John Murray. Available at: www.econlib.org/library/Ricardo/ricP.html.

Rimmer, B. 2009. "Slough estates in the 1990s: client-driven SCM". In S. Pryke (ed.), *Construction Supply Chain Management*, 137–59. Oxford: Wiley-Blackwell.

Robinson, J. & J. Eatwell 1973. *An Introduction to Modern Economics*. London: McGraw-Hill.

Shen, L.-Y., V. Tam, L. Tam & Y.-B. Ji 2010. "Project feasibility study: the key to successful implementation of sustainable and socially responsible construction management practice". *Journal of Cleaner Production* 18(3), 254–9.

Sherman, H. 2014. *The Business Cycle: Growth and Crisis under Capitalism*, reprint edn. Princeton, NJ: Princeton University Press.

Sithole, B. 2016. "Sources of disputes in South African construction contracts and the resolution techniques employed between clients and contractors". MSc dissertation, Faculty of Engineering and the Built Environment, University of the Witwatersrand. Available at: http://hdl.handle.net/10539/22337 (last accessed 1 July 2018).

Thorstein, V. 1904. *The Theory of Business Enterprise*. New York: Scribner's.

Von Neumann, J. & O. Morgenstern 1944. *Theory of Games and Economic Behavior*. Princeton, NJ: Princeton University Press.

Wallsten, S. 2015. *The Competitive Effects of the Sharing Economy: How Is Uber Changing Taxis?* Washington, DC: Technology Policy Institute.

Wu, J., M. Kumaraswamy & G. Soo 2008. "Payment problems and regulatory responses in the construction industry: mainland China perspective". *Journal of Professional Issues in Engineering Education and Practice* 134(4), 399–407.

Zervas, G., D. Proserpio & J. Byers 2017. "The rise of the sharing economy: estimating the impact of Airbnb on the hotel industry". *Journal of Marketing Research* 54(5), 687–705.

LIST OF FIGURES AND TABLES

Figures

1.1	UK gross fixed capital formation (2016)	3
1.2	Turnover in UK construction (2016)	4
1.3	Construction employment in the UK by size of firm (2016)	5
1.4	The number of firms in UK construction (2016)	6
1.5	The supply chain on a small project	7
1.6	The supply chain on a large project	8
1.7	UK construction output at current and constant prices (1997–2016)	11
1.8	UK construction output by sector (2016)	12
2.1	Simple supply and demand showing price equilibrium	18
2.2	The market mechanism	19
2.3	The equilibrium position of a firm in perfect competition	24
2.4	A monopoly	27
2.5	Index of UK imports and construction output (1983–2016)	29
2.6	UK imports of construction materials as a proportion of construction output (1983–2016)	30
3.1	Profit margins of the top ten UK house builders and building contractors (2015/16 & 2016/17)	38
5.1	UK productivity (2006–16)	78
5.2	UK productivity by sector (1996–2016)	78
5.3	Total productivity and marginal productivity	80
5.4	Productivity and wages	81
5.5	Supply and demand in the labour market	82
5.6	Productivity in UK manufacturing and construction (1996–2016)	88
5.7	Private housing starts in England (2001–17)	90
6.1	Average profit margin of the top ten UK contractors (2013/14–2016/17)	97
6.2	The prisoner's dilemma	101

6.3	The contractor's dilemma	103
6.4	The driver's choice	105
6.5	Clients and contractors	106
7.1	Costs including profits (millions)	112
7.2	Adding value to material inputs	113
7.3	Exchange value, value added and surplus value	114
7.4	The relationship between surplus and value added	117
8.1	The volatility in activity in the UK economy and construction (2007–17)	127
8.2	Employment in UK construction (2007–17)	129
8.3	The fall in UK construction employment by gender (2008–13)	130
8.4	UK construction employment by occupation and gender (12 months to September 2007 and September 2017)	132
8.5	Private house building in England (2001–16)	135
8.6	UK private housing output and new orders (1985–2017)	140
8.7	UK commercial building output and new orders (1985–2017)	141
8.8	UK infrastructure output and new orders (1985–2017)	143
9.1	The feasibility study: finding the missing value	157
9.2	Estimating the internal rate of return from the discounted cash flow table	164
9.3	The net cumulative cash flow of a project	165

Tables

1.1	The UK construction supply chain (2015)	9
3.1	Cost-plus pricing in construction	39
3.2	Definitions of the concepts used in the profit and loss account	45
3.3	The operating cycle	51
9.1	The discounted cash flow	161
10.1	A simplified balanced scorecard	178

INDEX

2012 London Olympics 96
3D printing 182

Abdel-Wahab, M. 85
accelerator principle 122
accountants 22
acid test 50
adjudication 99, 110
air-conditioning 5
Airbnb 31–2, 33
Ali, A. 74
arbitration 99, 110
architects 4
asset strippers 63, 64
Azhar, S. 181

Baiden, B. 86–7
balance sheet 44
balanced scorecard 176, 178
Barney, J. 70
barriers to entry 25
benefit–cost ratio 160, 164
Bhopal chemical plant disaster
    (1984) 155
bidding strategy 40
bill of quantities 39, 149
Blue Book, The 2
bonds, government 152
booms and slumps 119
bought-in work 42
Bowley, M. 149

Bowonder, B. 155
Bresnan, M. 75
Briscoe, G. 74
build to order 13, 133
builders' merchants 4, 5, 64, 117, 118
building
    contractors 9
    maintenance 173
    regulations 148
    specifications 149
building information modelling (BIM) 36,
    70, 71, 180–2
Building Regulations Act (UK) 2010 72
built environment 2
Burns, A. 124
business cycles 119, 120, 123–4
Byers, J. 32

Campbell, W. 97
capacity 123, 131
Capen, E. 97
capital 16
    consumption 122
    employed 46
    formation 2
    intensity 78–9
Carillion 51, 55–8, 133, 179
cash flow 35, 72, 173, 174
    difficulties 47, 49, 55
    management 49
cash reserves 125

CH2M Hill 172
Chang, C. 75
Channel Tunnel 142
civil engineering firms 6
Clapp, R. 97
commercial building 141
company growth, theory of 62
Competition and Markets Authority 27
competitive advantage 62–3
compound interest 162
compounding 162
Constructing Excellence 178
construction
 business cycles 125
 contracts 147
 employment 5, 128–9
 fragmented industry 14
 industry 11, 146
 innovation 68
 management 150–1
 market 61
 and new orders 138
 output 1, 11
 project management 171, 173, 174, 175
 and property markets 15
 team 145
construction sector
 output of 12
 structure of 12
consumer goods 122
contractors 167
 main 44, 74, 148
 management of 150–1
 specialist 71, 146–7
 traditional 148
contractor's dilemma 102–4
corporate social responsibility 168
cost, average 64
cost of sales 44
cost–benefit analyses 145
cost-plus pricing 39
counter-cyclical policies 120
credit cycles 121
creditor days 52
current assets 50
current liabilities 50
current prices 10

cycle amplitude 124
cycle base 124
cycle relative 124

Dainty, A. 74, 86–7
De Valence, G. 37
dead cat bounce 127
debtor days 52
decision criteria 160
default, risk of 179
delays 175
Delmar, F. 68
demand (and supply) 15–16
Department for Business, Energy and
 Industrial Strategy (BEIS) (UK) 2
depreciation 122–3
design and build 149–50
developer 145
digitized hydraulics 84
direct labour 111
discounted cash flow table 161, 163–4
discounting 161–2
disputes 41
 resolution 176
double counting 9
driver's choice 104–5
drones 84
Durdyev, S. 74
Dutch auction 43, 99, 168

earnings before interest and tax 45–6
economic rent 16, 115
economic viability 155
economies of scale 7, 64
economists 22
efficient level of output 64–5
English auction 95
enterprise 16
environmental policies 169
equilibrium
 price 17
 wage 83
exchange value 115

facilities management 173
factors of production 15
feasibility studies 145, 154–7, 159, 169

financial
  capitalists 116, 117
  management 44
  viability 154
financial crisis of 2008 12, 77
firm, growth of 66
first-price sealed-bid auction 95
fixed costs 23
fixed-price tendering 168
full cost pricing 35
future value 163

gearing 179
glass industry 8
Glenigan 178
Glick, S. 180
Grenfell Tower 136–8
gross fixed capital formation 2
gross profit 45–6
gross value added 8
Gruneberg, S. 52, 125, 147, 176, 178, 179
Guggemos, A. 180
guilds 61

head office costs 39
heating and ventilation 5
heavyside products 5
hedging 133
hedonic pricing 157
Hillebrandt, P. 54, 72
house-building sector 134–6
housing 122
  market 38, 88–92
  private 12
  output and new orders 140
Hughes, W. 54, 72, 147
Hyde, K. 73

Imports, of construction products 30
industrial capitalists 116
Industrial Revolution 61
inflation 10
information technology 36
infrastructure 12, 13, 143
intangible costs 155, 157
integrated project delivery (IPD) 180
integrated project management 36, 85, 86

interest payments 46, 49
internal rate of return (IR) 160, 163–4
internet 31
interstices 66
inventories 29, 120
investment 62
Ive, G. 75, 125

Jaafar, M. 74
Ji, J.-B. 168, 169
Joint Contracts Tribunal (JCT) 148
just in time (JIT) 37

Kadir, M. 74
key performance indicators 178
Khalfan, M. 181
Koskela, L. 37
Ku, K. 181
Kumaraswamy, M. 74

labour 16
  market 82
  productivity 78–9, 83, 92
labour intensive processes 79
Laing O'Rourke 172
landowning capitalists 116
late payment 72
Latham Report (1994) 151
law of diminishing returns 24–5, 80
law of supply 17
lead role 175
leading indicators 121
lean construction 37, 85–6
lean manufacturing 37
lean production 37
Lee, W. 74
lightside products 5
liquidity 52
  ratios 179
litigation 99, 110
London Olympic Games 152, 172
  supply chain 176
Loosemore, M. 87, 176

Mace 173
managers 68
Maqsood, T. 181

marginal cost 23, 167
  cost pricing 35, 36
  prime costs 35
  and productivity 79
  revenue 23, 167
market
  failure 18, 169
  price 19
  testing 26
mark-up 35, 39, 40
Marshall, N. 75
mass production 64
maximax 101
maximin 101
maximum negative cash flow 160, 164
Mbachu, J. 74
McKelvie, A. 68
Mead, J. 176, 178, 179
mediation 99, 110
men in construction 130–2
merchant capitalists 117
mergers 44
micro-firms 6
Millett, S. 74
Mitchell, W. 124
Monopolies and Mergers Commission
    (UK) 27
monopoly 26–7
Monthly Business Survey (for
    Construction and Allied Trades) 10
moral hazard 153
Morgenstern, O. 100
multiplier 122
Murdoch, I. 52
Murdoch, J. 54, 72

Nash equilibrium 102
national debt 152
National Planning Policy Framework 148
negotiation 76
net cumulative cash flow 165
net current assets 50
net discounted present value 160–1,
    165
net investment 123
net profit margin 46
net profits after tax 46

new engineering contract 152
non-price competition 28

Office for National Statistics (ONS) 8
office surplus 20
off-site manufacturing 88–92
Ogunmola, P. 76
Oke, A. 76
oligopoly 27–8
Olympic Delivery Authority (ODA)
    96, 172
Olympic Delivery Partner, CLM 172, 174
one-way discussions 179
open-ascending bid auction 95
operating cycle 51, 53
opportunity cost 67
overdraft facility 49
overhead costs 45, 46

Pareto optimality 160
Pareto, V. 159
partnering agreements 74, 151
payback period 160, 165
pay when paid clauses 52, 75
Penrose, E. 66
perfect knowledge 21
perfectly competitive market 21
performance ratios 179
plant and tool hire 4, 33
  firms 5
porosity of the working day 83
portfolio of projects 43, 173
positive cash flow 42, 52
power asymmetry 98
present value 163, 164
Price, A. 85, 86–7
price maker 26
prime costs 39, 42, 133
prisoner's dilemma 100–1
private commercial 12
Private Finance Initiative (PFI) 152
private industrial 12
procurement 147, 148
product
  manufacturers 4
  markets 69
production 114

productivity 2, 77, 84
  growth 84
profit 110, 111, 114
  after tax 45
  margin 38, 40–1, 42, 48, 54, 62, 69, 168, 172
  -maximizing firms 25
  -maximizing level 167
  ratios 179
profit and loss account 44
projects 147
  management 173
  partnering contracts 152
  vision 176
Proserpio, D. 32
public sector (non-housing) 13
public–private partnerships (PPP) 152

quantity surveying 149
Quirke, J. 84

Ramachandra, T. 73
rate of return 45–6, 165
Raworth, K. 62
recessions 119, 127
rent 49
repair, maintenance and improvement (RM&I) 12
resource-based view (RBV) 70
retention 72, 76, 98
  payments 53, 54
revenue, average 23
Rimmer, B. 175
risk 14, 26, 147
  aversion 101
  management 173, 175
  preferences 101
Rotimi, J. 73

Sapuan, S. 74
self-propelled management robots 84
share price 46
Shen, L.-Y. 168, 169
Sherman, H. 124
shortages 18
simple interest 162
site acquisition 166

site options 166
Sithole, B. 109
size of project 167
small- and medium-sized enterprises (SMEs) 3
snags 166
soft management issues 75
Soo, G. 74
spare capacity 65, 67
speculative building 13, 37, 134, 153
speculative developers 167
stakeholders 116, 158
steel industry 8
subcontracting 6, 7, 172
subcontractors 32–3, 87, 147
supply chain 1, 4, 175, 176
surplus value 110, 111, 115, 116
surpluses 18
sustainability 62, 176

Taiebat, M. 181
Tam, L. 168, 169
Tam, V. 168, 169
tangible costs 155
temporary construction teams 86, 87, 182
tendering 38–40
  bids 168
  documents 149, 177
  process 149
tier 1 contractors 176
time value of money 158
total cost 23
total factor productivity 85
total quality management (TQM) 37
total revenue 23
Town and Country Planning Act (UK) 1990 148
trust, lack of 75
turnover 54
two-way discussions 179

Uber 31–2, 33
UK National Accounts 2
utilitarianism 159

value added 8, 111, 113
value of the marginal product 81

variable cost 22
Vogl, B. 85
void periods 166
von Neumann, J. 100
VRIN characteristics 70

wages 82
warranty period 148
weighted importance rating system 176
Wennberg, K. 68

winner's curse 97
women in construction 130–2
work packages 26, 147
working capital 35, 47, 49–50, 51,
    53, 72, 73
    requirement 50, 53
Wu, J. 74

zero-sum game 100, 110
Zervas, G. 32